THE ESTATES OF OLD TORONTO

THE ESTATES OF OLD TORONTO

LIZ LUNDELL

The BOSTON MILLS PRESS

For Kate & Owen, with love.

Published in 1997 by
Boston Mills Press
132 Main Street
Erin, Ontario, Canada N0B 1T0
Tel 519-833-2407
Fax 519-833-2195
www.boston-mills.on.ca

Distributed in Canada by
General Distribution Services Limited
30 Lesmill Road
Toronto, Canada M3B 2T6
Tel 416-445-3333
Fax 416-445-5967
e-mail customer.service@ccmailgw.genpub.com

Distributed in the United States by
General Distribution Services Inc.
85 River Rock Drive, Suite 202
Buffalo, New York 14207
Toll-free 1-800-805-1083
Fax 416-445-5967
e-mail customer.service@ccmailgw.genpub.com

01 00 99 98 97   1 2 3 4 5

CATALOGING IN PUBLICATION DATA

Lundell, Liz, 1959–
The estates of Old Toronto

Includes bibliographical references and index.
ISBN 1-55046-219-9

1. Country homes–Ontario–Toronto–History. 2. Historic buildings–Ontario–
Toronto. 3. Architecture, Domestic–Ontario–Toronto–History. 4. Toronto
(Ont.)–Buildings, structures, etc. 5. Toronto (Ont.)–History. I. Title.

FC3097.7L86 1997   971.3'541   C97-932106-9
F1059.5.T688 1997

Editing by James Bosma
Design by Gillian Stead
Map design by Mary Firth
Printed in Canada

CONTENTS

ACKNOWLEDGMENTS

Preparing this book has been a humbling activity. Several inimitable studies of Toronto have made great contributions to our understanding of local history, and I cannot dream of approaching the depth of research that they represent. In particular, this book is indebted to the work of Eric Arthur, J. M. S. Careless, William Dendy, Edith Firth, William Kilbourn, and Lucy Booth Martyn.

Many people provided assistance in research and in locating photography for this book. I would like to thank Gabriella Karadi and Joan Crosbie of the Toronto Historical Board; Lynda Moon and Barbara Myrvold of the Toronto Public Library; Albert Fulton and Keith Miller of Wychwood Park Archives; Brother Donald Morgan, De La Salle College Oaklands; Alan Walker, Metropolitan Toronto Reference Library; Steve MacKinnon, City of Toronto Archives; Hélène Van Houte, Glendon College, York University; Linda Gray, Crescent School; Jeanne Hopkins, North York Public Library; Steven Bell, Culture Branch, North York Parks and Recreation; Katherine Kossuth, Canadian Film Centre; Gord Benner, Metropolitan Toronto Transportation; John Niedra, Public Works, City of Toronto; Carol Baum, Royal Ontario Museum; Joan Kinsella; Stephen Otto; Mike Filey; Bill and Carol Gray; Don Ritchie; and the staffs of the Ontario Archives, the Toronto Public Library, and the Special Collections Department at the Metropolitan Toronto Reference Library.

The people who preserve the existing homes, either as public buildings or as private residences, deserve appreciation. Special thanks to owners and descendants who offered tours or provided photographs, in particular Dorothy Bullen, Win Burry, Marianne Rogers, Guy Saunders, and Mary Sinclair.

The gang at Boston Mills Press is always a joy to work with. John Denison, who continues to do so much for heritage studies, came up for the idea for this book. Thanks also to Noel Hudson, Kathy Fraser, James Bosma, and Gill Stead for making the end product look so good and for making the whole process a lot of fun.

Don Standfield, as always, was very generous with his time and encouragement and provided excellent photographs of existing buildings. Thanks to Mary Firth for bringing order to very chaotic geographic jottings and for producing the maps.

Many other friends suggested contacts and took an interest in the project, and, although they are too numerous to mention by name, I have appreciated their ongoing support. Thanks especially to Elma.

Finally, I would like to thank Guy, our children, and their grandparents for continuing to encourage me in my writing and in so many other ways.

Perhaps Toronto's best-known estate, Casa Loma was unparalleled in opulence.
The three sets of bronze doors to the conservatory were replicas of gates in an Italian palace. Each pair cost $10,000.
Photograph courtesy Casa Loma.

INTRODUCTION

A cooling breeze rushes forward carrying delicate birdsong from the leafy incline ahead, while laughter bubbles from a hidden swimming hole. Cattle sprawl beneath swaying elms and the city drops far behind, a hazy outline topped by church spires. Up the winding drive, a rustle of long skirts, and then the muffled crunch of gravel underfoot heralds arrival at the country estate. Unhurried pursuits await. Perhaps a stroll through the gardens, or tea and relaxed conversation on the terrace. There is a sense of leisure, a pervading air of calm.

Time has transformed Toronto since Lieutenant-Governor John Graves Simcoe selected the site of York to be the capital of fledgling Upper Canada in 1793, yet many features that exist today are lasting reminders of Toronto's early landholders and their estates. These estates were sizeable country properties with impressive homes. Often a working farm occupied part of the lot, but even if not, the houses were adorned with gardens, orchards, and lawns and equipped with stables, outbuildings, and imposing gates.

As the town grew, affluent residents would build their gracious pastoral retreats always just beyond the city's boundaries. D'Arcy Boulton Jr. built the Grange in dense forest just west of modern University Avenue. The escarpment above Davenport Road drew other families because of the clear air and commanding views of the city and Lake Ontario.

A few of the old homes remain, including Colborne Lodge, Spadina, and the Grange, but most of the large estates were subdivided during the last century. The landscaped gardens, winding carriage drives, and grand residences disappeared as residential and commercial areas spread out from the city centre. Where gentleman farmers once rambled across fields on horseback, busy commercial developments stand today. Orchards have given way to office towers. Tree-lined laneways have grown to six-lane arteries with subterranean transit service.

Here is a bittersweet look back at a less harried age, before these large properties were swallowed up by the city. These estates were part of a privileged, composed lifestyle that could not last; yet the image still has the power to engage our modern, urban sensibilities. A few of these estates have survived. For those that have not, street names and other reminders point to Toronto's large estates and the families who owned them. The estates of Old Toronto have left their enduring imprint on our city.

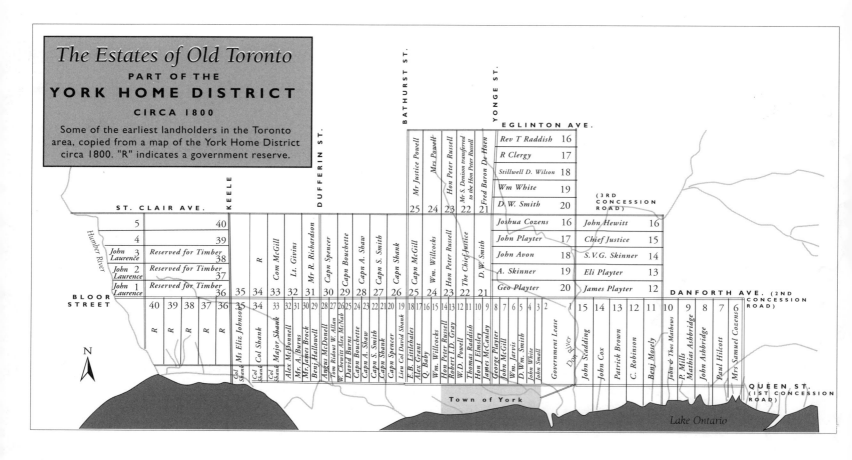

A copy of the earliest land grants in the Home District of York, showing landholders, circa 1800.
The park lots run north from the first concession, Lot Street (now Queen), up to the second concession (now Bloor).

The Ashbridge home, at 1444 Queen Street East, built in 1854.

From *Toronto Then and Now*, by J. Clarence Duff and Sarah Yates, published by Fitzhenry & Whiteside. Sketch reproduced with permission of Cairn Capitol Inc.

LAYING FOUNDATIONS FOR A CITY

When John Graves Simcoe arrived at the beginning of the long-used Toronto Portage to the Upper Great Lakes, the site was home to just one fur trader. Simcoe had already established a temporary capital at Niagara. Kingston was also under serious consideration, but, in 1793, the first lieutenant-governor selected this spot for a garrison and the seat of government for the newly formed province of Upper Canada, naming it York for the British commanding general, the Duke of York.

The site was ideal for military purposes: it had a well-protected natural harbour, good farmland beyond, excellent timber reserves for shipbuilding, and a route to the Holland River, Lake Simcoe, and Georgian Bay, by way of the Humber River.

The first major landholder was, of course, the military. A small garrison was built beside Garrison Creek, at modern Bathurst Street and Lakeshore Boulevard. At the same time, Simcoe set aside large government and clergy reserves, including an area bounded by the Don River, modern Carlton and Parliament Streets, and the lake, for use as a shipyard. He ordered that two military trails be cut out of the dense forest north of the new town. One, stretching west to the Humber, Simcoe named for Cabinet Minister Sir Henry Dundas; the second, running north, he named for his friend, and Secretary of War at the time, Sir George Yonge.

The original survey laid out the familiar rectangular grids and concessions that still exist today. The base line for the survey was Lot Street, today's Queen Street. Lots close to the lake had a north–south orientation, while those closer to the Don and Humber Rivers ran east to west to take advantage of water access. Beyond that, the rigid grid system paid little attention to topography, completely ignoring the many ravines. It is easy to see on a modern map how the orientation of Toronto's major routes is bound to that original survey. It is also easy to identify tracks that predated the original survey by their curved routes. Davenport Road, Poplar Plains Road, and the original carrying trail (now Highway 400) along the Humber River were all established by Indians long before the surveys of the 1790s.

The town of York was situated just west of the mouth of the Don River. Originally it was laid out in one-acre lots, occupying ten blocks between modern Jarvis and Parliament Streets. In 1797, it expanded with the addition of the "New Town" from Jarvis to Peter Street and the land north to Lot Street.

All early officials were granted parcels of land, both town and outlying lots, as remuneration in accordance with rank. For example, a member of the Executive Council received a total of six thousand acres. A United Empire Loyalist was entitled to twelve hundred acres himself and the same for his spouse and each child.

Just beyond Lot Street was a string of hundred-acre park lots that stretched one and a quarter miles north to the present Bloor Street. As Simcoe wrote to Dundas in 1794, the park lots "were so laid out as to give one hundred acres to each of the Officers of the Government as an inducement to build an House in the town & a remuneration for its expence…." From the outset, the park lots were intended to support a landed aristocracy in York. Simcoe hoped they would be developed along the lines of English estates, where the country house represented social status and a source of significant wealth.

Lord Selkirk suggested in his diary of 1803 that Simcoe had selected York over Kingston "partly because Lord Dorchester approved of it, but principally because all of the lands were taken up around it — York had the advantage of being able to afford lots for all his friends round it, accordingly the lands for some miles distance are all in the hands of Officers of the Government…." Most of the park lots were granted in September 1793, and Simcoe's influence is obvious in a partial list of patentees: Peter Russell, Receiver General; William Jarvis, Simcoe's civil secretary; John Scadding, Simcoe's Devonshire estate manager; Dr. James Macaulay, surgeon to Simcoe's regiment; and Major John Small, Clerk of the Executive Council.

In 1800, York's population had reached only four hundred, and few houses had been built on the park lots. Some of the owners sold firewood to clear the southern parts of their properties and a few sold off parcels, but it was often the next generation that made fortunes and erected elegant homes.

At the time of Toronto's incorporation, in 1834, there were approximately nine thousand inhabitants within the city, which was bounded roughly by Parliament, Bathurst, Dundas, and Lake Ontario. By that time, many owners of the original two-hundred-acre farm lots north of Bloor had started to improve their estates, as had owners both east and west of the city proper. Although the first estate owners had been members of the military or political elite, it was the dry goods merchants, railway barons, and power magnates who erected fine residences during the Victorian age.

In 1850, during an economic boom and with a population of approximately thirty thousand, Toronto expanded to Bloor Street. The 1850s also saw the first subdivision of many of the city's large estates, including Moss Park, the Crookshank Estate, and the Denisons' Bellevue. The railway provided a boost to development in the middle of the century as well, encouraging expansion and forcing the successful commercial men of the late 1800s to purchase property farther out of the city for their country mansions.

In the 1880s, a tax exemption for lawns and gardens was repealed, further encouraging subdivision. The physical area of the city more than doubled during the last two decades of the century as the city gobbled up suburban villages through annexation: Yorkville in 1883; Riverdale and Brockton in 1884; Rosedale and the Annex in 1887; Seaton Village and Sunnyside in 1888; and Parkdale in 1889. By 1901, Toronto's population had grown to 235,000. Development continued to encroach upon the estates at the edge of the city as rising prices and improved transportation spurred growth.

The last large estates on Toronto's fringe were built during the 1920s along Bayview Avenue. Although these estates are outside Toronto proper, they are included in this book as examples of the type of large properties — complete with grand homes and expansive grounds — that once covered much of the area.

THE ESTATES

CASTLE FRANK
The Simcoes

Crossing the Prince Edward Viaduct from the east and looking just slightly south, you can see a tree-covered ridge that overlooks the Don Valley. Wild rice once grew in the river below, attracting geese every fall, and fishing parties would travel up from the lake by canoe to catch salmon. In 1793, the Simcoes began to build a summer home on the crest of this ridge. They named the home Castle Frank, for their son, Francis.

In town, the family had been living in large canvas tents, several purchased from the effects of explorer Captain James Cook. Castle Frank was a more permanent home, but it was never intended for use as a primary residence. Despite this, it is arguably Toronto's first country estste.

Simcoe secured a patent in his young son's name. On October 29, 1794, Elizabeth Simcoe made the following entry in her diary:

> The Govr having determined to take a lot of 200 acres upon the River Donn for Francis, & the Law obliges persons having Lots of Land to build a House upon them within a year — we went today to fix upon the spot for building his House — we went 6 miles by water & landed, climbed up an exceeding steep hill or rather a series of sugar loafed Hills & approved of the highest spot from where we looked down on the tops of large trees & seeing Eagles near I suppose they build there — there are large Pine plains around it which being without underwood & can ride or walk on, & we hope the height of the situation will secure us from Musquetos...."

In the midst of the original white pine, elm, basswood, and butternut forest, the house was a sizeable thirty-by-fifty-foot pine-log structure "built on the plan of a Greek Temple," as Elizabeth described it. Sixteen-foot pillars made of peeled pine logs supported imposing porticoes on either end. There were four windows along each side and a centre chimney, although the interior was never finished. From the little clearing in front of the building, the soldiers cut a carriage road to town. That road is part of today's Parliament Street.

Elizabeth used Castle Frank as a summerhouse and country retreat, going up the Don by sleigh in winter or through the woods in summer for picnics and parties. Early Toronto's noted historian Henry Scadding mused in *Toronto of Old*:

> We can picture to ourselves the cavalcade that was wont from time to time, to be seen in the summers and autumns of 1794–'5–'6, wending its leisurely way to the romantically situated chateau of Castle Frank along the reaches and windings, the descents and ascents of the forest road, expressly cut out through the primitive woods as a means of access to it.

There was a February cariole trip up the river, upon which Mrs. Simcoe entertained her friends Mrs. Macaulay and Miss Crookshank. In April 1796, when Francis was ill, Elizabeth took the children to Castle Frank for a change of air. She observed:

> The Porticos are delightful pleasant & the Room cool from its height & the thickness of the logs from which the House is built — the Mountain Tea berries in great perfection — Francis is much better & busy in planting Currant bushes & Peach trees....

Elizabeth Posthuma (Gwillim) Simcoe (1762–1850). Based on a watercolour by Mary Anne Burges, this painting shows Elizabeth as a young woman in Welsh dress just shortly before she accompanied the Governor to Upper Canada. Metropolitan Toronto Reference Library T30840

*Castle Frank, from a drawing by
Elizabeth Simcoe, circa 1794.
"Built on the plan of a Greek Temple,"
as Mrs. Simcoe explained in her diary,
Castle Frank stood on a ridge on the west
side of the Don River, south of modern
Bloor Street East.* MTRL JRR T11502

Simcoe returned to England in 1796 due to ill health. Peter Russell used the property after the Simcoe's departure, and Russell's friend, John Denison, occupied the house on his arrival at York. Simcoe died en route to Gibraltar in October 1806, and Castle Frank was closed the same year. Francis never returned to his estate. He attended Eton, joined the military at age seventeen, and was killed in action in Spain four years later in April 1812.

During the invasion of York, American troops travelled up the Don in search of Castle Frank, which was indicated on one of their maps. They assumed it would be a grand building and perhaps the central headquarters of the government — a true castle. But by that time Castle Frank was nothing more than an abandoned, rotting log cabin. Careless fishermen burned Castle Frank to the ground in 1829, and the Simcoe family gradually sold off their property in Upper Canada.

After Simcoe left, John Scadding managed the estate and purchased a portion of the land. In 1844, John Scadding Jr. and his wife, Amelia, donated part of the property for St. James Cemetery. Much later, Sir Edward Kemp built a second, twenty-four-room Castle Frank, north of the original site. It was demolished in 1962 to make way for the present Rosedale Heights Secondary School. Today, a road, a crescent, and a subway stop perpetuate the name of Castle Frank.

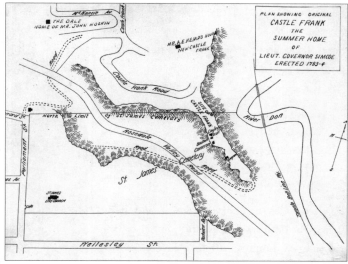

*Attributed to Owen Staples and drawn for John Ross Robertson's
"Landmarks of Toronto" series in the* Evening Telegram,
*this plan shows the Castle Frank site circa 1900.
By that time, most of the estate had become St. James Cemetery.
Kemp's new Castle Frank stands north of the Simcoe house.
The building at the top of Parliament Street was most likely
the Player gate lodge.* MTRL T14122

PETERSFIELD
Peter Russell

Peter Russell, born in Cork in 1731, was the only son of an army captain. He had a liberal education and then secured a commission in the army. Russell supported his penniless father and his half-sister, Elizabeth, for a number of years, but he was forced to sell his commission in order to pay mounting gambling debts. Russell met John Graves Simcoe in England in 1790. Simcoe offered to recommend Russell for a position in Upper Canada as Receiver General and Auditor and told Russell that although the salary was rather modest he would receive large land grants. At age fifty-nine, Russell set off with Elizabeth for Upper Canada.

Russell first built a house in town in 1797. Because of his position, he was entitled to another six thousand acres in other grants. He acquired park lot 14, between present-day Beverley and Huron Streets, where he soon built a substantial farmhouse at the head of modern-day Peter Street and established a very profitable farm named Petersfield.

Russell wrote to a cousin in May 1799:

> I have at last cleared about thirty Acres of my farm at the Expence of about Six Guineas the Acre & hope to draw some provisions from it next year for the Hay of last Winter cost me above £ 100....

Elizabeth took care of the flower and herb gardens at both residences, and journals of the day refer to the pretty arbours she created with many non-native plants such as lilacs, bachelor's buttons, and "snowball trees." The Russells divided their time between their town house and their country home.

After Simcoe left in 1796, Russell was the highest ranking official of both the Executive and Legislative Councils, and he acted as Administrator of Upper Canada until 1799. During that period, he enjoyed "a plurality of offices which would have been an inspiration to Gilbert and Sullivan," as Lucy Booth Martyn put it.

Russell was very successful in encouraging friends and relatives to join him in Upper Canada. He persuaded a cousin, William Willcocks, the debt-ridden mayor of Cork, to settle in York, where he became a merchant, magistrate, and postmaster. Willcocks persuaded another Irish family, the Baldwins, to relocate to York. Russell also convinced John Denison, a friend from Yorkshire, to emigrate. Denison eventually managed the Petersfield property. Wrote Henry Scadding:

> Our own recollection of Mrs. Denison is associated with Petersfield, the homely cosiness of whose interior, lighted up by a rousing fire of great logs, piled high in one of the capacious and lofty fireplaces of the time, made an indelible impression.

The landed class in York was insular and cliquish. Entries in the diary of Joseph Willcocks indicate just how tightly knit York society was in 1800. Within the space of a few weeks, Willcocks had tea at the Russells, called at the McGills and Jarvises with Elizabeth Russell, and received calls from George Playter, Mr. Ridout, John Denison, William Allan, and Dr. William W. Baldwin. This group, all of whom owned impressive estates, would have an enduring influence on the character of the city.

The Honourable Peter Russell (1731–1808) came to Upper Canada plagued by debts. Through Simcoe's patronage, he was promoted to Receiver General. After Simcoe's return to England, Russell acted as President and Administrator until 1799. MTRL JRR T34630

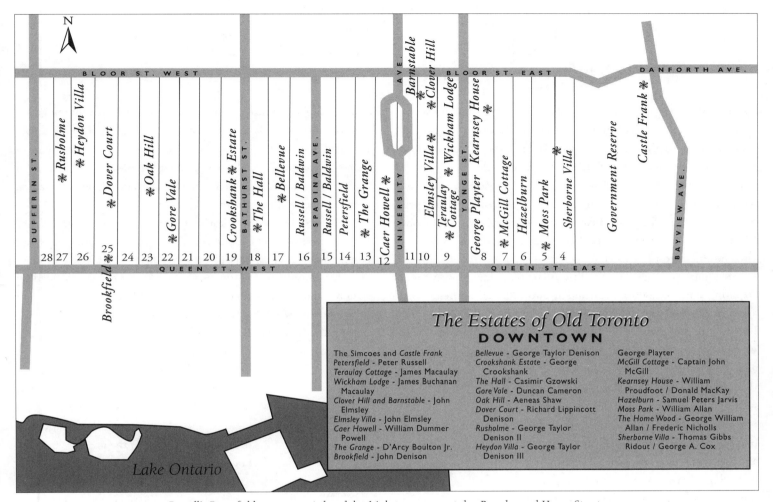

The Estates of Old Toronto
DOWNTOWN

The Simcoes and *Castle Frank*
Petersfield - Peter Russell
Teraulay Cottage - James Macaulay
Wickham Lodge - James Buchanan
  Macaulay
Clover Hill and Barnstable - John
  Elmsley
Elmsley Villa - John Elmsley
Caer Howell - William Dummer
  Powell
The Grange - D'Arcy Boulton Jr.
Brookfield - John Denison

Bellevue - George Taylor Denison
Crookshank Estate - George
  Crookshank
The Hall - Casimir Gzowski
Gore Vale - Duncan Cameron
Oak Hill - Aeneas Shaw
Dover Court - Richard Lippincott
  Denison
Rusholme - George Taylor
  Denison II
Heydon Villa - George Taylor
  Denison III

George Playter
McGill Cottage - Captain John
  McGill
Kearnsey House - William
  Proudfoot / Donald MacKay
Hazelburn - Samuel Peters Jarvis
Moss Park - William Allan
The Home Wood - George William
  Allan / Frederic Nicholls
Sherborne Villa - Thomas Gibbs
  Ridout / George A. Cox

Russell's Petersfield estate occupied park lot 14, between present-day Beverley and Huron Streets.
Russell later added two lots on the west, extending his very profitable farm almost to modern Augusta Avenue.

Peter Russell retired in 1800 and added to his considerable landholdings with shrewd purchases. He purchased park lots 15 and 16, to the west of Petersfield, in the early 1800s. By the time he died, in 1808, he had acquired a great deal of property in and around York, which Elizabeth inherited. As she never married, in spite of at least two serious proposals, upon her death in 1822 most of the property went to her two cousins, Phoebe Willcocks Baldwin and Maria Willcocks. Phoebe's husband, Dr. Baldwin, was executor.

A short street between Sherbourne and Princess, south of King, is named Abbey Lane for the Russells' town house, Russell Abbey. Bedford Road was named for the Duke of Bedford, patriarch of the Russell family. Although the Petersfield house was still standing in 1872, no pictures survive today. Russell Hill Road is another visible reminder of the large landholdings of the influential administrator.

TERAULAY COTTAGE
James Macaulay

James Macaulay was born in Scotland in 1759, and he was a surgeon with Simcoe's regiment during the American Revolution. John Graves Simcoe commended Macaulay as "a young man attached to his Profession, and of that docile, patient, and industrious turn ... that will willingly direct itself to any pursuit." In 1792, Simcoe asked Macaulay to accompany him to Niagara and from there to York. Elizabeth Hayter, whom Macaulay married in 1790, was a childhood friend of Elizabeth Simcoe, and the two ladies frequently exchanged visits during the early years at York.

Macaulay, as Surgeon to the British Forces, assiduously set about acquiring land — 1,600 acres including a town lot for himself, 1,200 acres for Elizabeth, and 660 acres for each of his children. The most important grant, received in 1797, was park lot 9, a hundred acres west of modern Yonge Street, between Queen and Bloor Streets. At some point after 1818, the Macaulays and their neighbours to the west, the Elmsleys, decided to exchange portions of their park lots so that both properties would have Yonge Street frontage and be a quarter mile wide. The Elmsleys, preferring higher ground, took the portion north of present-day College Street. The Macaulays chose the southern parcel that was closer to town. Both Elmsley and Macaulay were strong proponents of opening and improving Yonge Street, which was nothing more than a muddy track throughout most of their tenure.

The Macaulay home, named Teraulay Cottage, stood where Holy Trinity Church now stands. The name came either from the Gaelic *ter,* meaning land or a combination of James and Elizabeth's surnames. The Macaulays later laid out York's first working-class subdivision, northwest of today's Yonge and Queen Streets, on their land. Many of the streets in the area — James, Elizabeth, Hayter, Edward, Louisa, Teraulay, Jeremy, Anne, and Hagarman — bear family names.

Elizabeth died in 1809, leaving four sons and four daughters. The doctor married Rachel Crookshank, sister of George Crookshank and another member of Elizabeth Simcoe's circle.

After a twelve-year posting to Quebec City, where he was medical examiner and established military hospitals, Macaulay retired to York on half pay in 1817. He served as senior medical officer from 1819 until his death in 1822.

The doctor left all of his property to his children and £2,000 in Bank of England stock to his widow. When he married, the eldest son, John Simcoe Macaulay, godson of John Graves Simcoe, received the homestead and the southern portion of the property fronting Lot Street. The second son, James Buchanan, received a large parcel at the north edge of the estate, where he built Wickham Lodge.

The sons continued subdividing the estate around their impressive homes. The surrounding subdivision was known as Macaulaytown, and it was annexed to the city in 1834 as St. Patrick's Ward. Largely filled with working-class housing, it had a population of 1,472 by that time. Fifteen years later, "The Ward," as it had come to be

A map of John Simcoe Macaulay's estate in 1845. Macaulay had left for England by this time and the lots were being sold off by agents. Shortly afterward, Macaulay presented property for Holy Trinity Church — the first Anglican church in Canada with free pews. MTRL

Alex Hamilton and family posing in the garden of Teraulay Cottage after it was sold and moved slightly north to make way for Holy Trinity Church (date unknown). The Eaton Centre now covers most of the Macaulays' country estate. City of Toronto Archives SC 203 #1

called, was composed of narrow alleys lined with sweatshops and dilapidated slum housing and crowded with immigrants who had fled rebellions, famine, and persecution in Europe.

John Macaulay was back in Britain by 1825, but he returned to Upper Canada in 1835 to manage his inheritance. A few years later, John and his wife, Ann, were living at Elmsley Villa with their four sons and five daughters. After suffering a number of political failures, he and the family left Upper Canada for good in 1843, leaving the remaining lots for sale through agents. The entire estate was sold off within ten years at a profit of about £21,000. John Simcoe Macaulay

died on his Kent estate in 1855.

A number of years before he died, Macaulay presented the Teraulay property to the Anglican Church to serve Toronto's poor. Teraulay Cottage was moved slightly north, and Holy Trinity church was built on the site, opening in 1847 as the first Anglican church in Canada with free pews.

Slowly, in the second half of the 1800s, Macaulaytown was built up. Many of its decrepit rooming houses were replaced with factories built by the T. Eaton Company. The Eaton Centre now occupies much of the Macaulays' original country estate.

Wickham Lodge, Sir James Buchanan Macaulay's residence, in the mid-1800s.
The house stood south of today's College Street, east of Bay. MTRL JRR T11385

WICKHAM LODGE
James Buchanan Macaulay

The second son of Dr. James Macaulay and Elizabeth Hayter was James Buchanan Macaulay, born in Niagara in 1793. James was educated at Dr. Strachan's school at Cornwall. He gained a commission in the 98th Regiment and served with distinction as an officer during the War of 1812. Law studies followed, and in 1822 he was called to the bar. In 1821, he married Rachel Gamble; they had one son and four daughters. By 1829, James Buchanan Macaulay, having distinguished himself as a fair and intelligent man, was appointed to the Queen's Bench.

After his father's death in 1822, James inherited a ten-acre square of the family estate, just north of his brother John's property. The parcel, south of College, was bounded roughly by modern Yonge and Bay Streets. Around 1841, Macaulay built Wickham Lodge, named for the Hampshire village of his forefathers, on the estate. Wickham was a two-storey Regency villa. Three tall windows on the second storey punctuated the brickwork. On the ground floor was a large drawing room with pretty views of lawns and gardens to the east and south. The house was set back from the dense pine forests along Yonge Street, and carriages entered the long horseshoe-shaped drive from Yonge, as College was a private road used exclusively by the University of Toronto.

From 1849 to 1856, Macaulay was Chief Justice of Common Pleas. He was knighted in 1859, just a short time before his death.

Throughout his career, James Macaulay heard a considerable number of cases and served on several law commissions. His reports were admired for their intelligence and fairness. He was also committed to providing relief for the less fortunate. Macauley died of heart failure at Osgoode Hall on the day he was reelected Treasurer of the Law Society.

Sir James died in 1859, leaving Wickham Lodge and an estate worth $40,000 to his wife. Lady Macaulay changed the spelling of the family home to Wykeham. Some time later she left for England, where she lived with one of her married daughters until her death in 1883.

In 1869, the family sold the property to Bishop Strachan School, which had been housed prior to that in the palatial residence of the late Bishop Strachan. The school moved into Wykeham Hall in 1870. Bishop Strachan School sold off some of the Yonge Street frontage during a building boom in the 1880s, financing several enlargements and alterations. After forty-five years, the school sold the property and moved to the present Lonsdale campus.

The Macaulay house served as a convalescent hospital for a time during the First World War, and later as the College Street Armouries. But the T. Eaton Company later bought the vacant house and remaining property and demolished the building. It opened its College Street store on the site in 1930. A few streets in the area were named for the Macaulays — Agnes (for a daughter), Teraulay, and Hayter — but most have disappeared with development.

The drawing room at Wykeham Hall, circa 1915.
From 1870 to 1915, the former Macaulay estate was home to Bishop Strachan School. MTRL T11389

CLOVER HILL AND BARNSTABLE
John Elmsley

The Elmsley's were another prominent family of landholders in York. The patriarch was the Honourable John Elmsley, Chief Justice of Upper Canada from 1796 to 1802. Elmsley was one of the few university-educated officials in the province, and according to Edith Firth in *The Canadian Dictionary of Biography*, was "much given to elegant phrases and Latin quotations, a habit that may not have endeared him to all his colleagues." Although he was reappointed Chief Justice of Lower Canada in 1802, Elmsley was in York long enough to amass more than eight thousand acres of land, including an impressive town residence — Elmsley House — a number of large parcels in York Township, and park lot 9. Rumours circulated that the Chief Justice had acquired his property by paying as little as a gallon of rum to a top price of £6 for a two-hundred-acre farm lot.

When the Chief Justice died in Montreal in 1805, the majority of the park lot parcel went intact to his sole male heir, Captain John Elmsley. Born in York in 1801, the Captain had served in the Navy, returned from England in 1827, farmed the family estate for a period, and then taken postings as captain on Great Lakes merchant and armed vessels.

John Elmsley built his first home, Clover Hill, on the northern portion of the Elmsley park lot in 1829. The house, facing east, was at the northeast corner of today's Bay and Joseph Streets, and much of the estate was shaded by mature oaks that thrived in the sandy soil. The lane (now St. Joseph Street) that entered

through the gate lodge, with its quaint diamond-lattice windows, was known for some time as Clover Hill Road. While the house was under construction, John lived in a log outbuilding that was later refurbished into a modest home appropriately named Barnstable.

In 1831, John Elmsley married Charlotte Sherwood, daughter of Chief Justice Henry Sherwood. Charlotte was a Catholic, and after a period of intense religious questioning, Elmsley converted to Roman Catholicism himself. In August 1833, he wrote a letter to the Bishop of Kingston. Enclosed was a cheque for £10 along with the following directions: "to be applied to suit charitable purposes as you may see fit." He confessed: "it is somewhere about the sum whereof I have, from time to time, defrauded my neighbours by wickedly shooting their swine, poultry and other property which I found on my farm." He further explained, "[it is] with the most hearty joy and satisfaction that I acquaint your Lordship of my intention of returning to the bosom of the Catholic Church from which my forefathers went forth in an evil hour…." It seems Elmsley was a rather impulsive character. A debate he later had with John Strachan about transubstantiation caused an uproar in Anglican York.

Around 1837, Elmsley built Elmsley Villa on the southern portion of his property, but in 1846 he was back at Clover Hill. Elmsley Villa was rented out until that portion of the property was sold in the 1850s.

John and Charlotte had ten children — seven boys and three

Clover Hill in 1909, when it was occupied by James Richardson.
By this time, the former Elmsley house stood at the northeast corner of St. Joseph and Bay Streets. MTRL JRR T11449

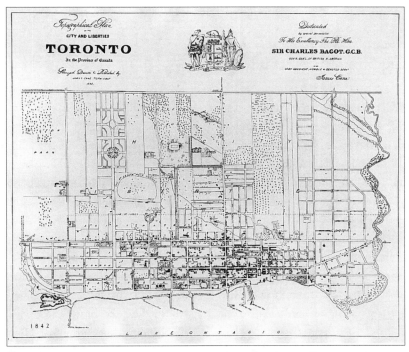

The drive to Wickham Lodge enters from Yonge Street just south of College and circles in front of the house. The carriageway to Teraulay Cottage also enters from Yonge just south of the city limits. Elmsley Villa, Barnstable, and Clover Hill appear on the plan farther up Yonge Street.
From the *Topographical Plan of the City and Liberties,* by James Cane (1842).

girls — although only two survived him, a daughter and a son. The daughter became a nun, and the son, Remegius, remained to live on the property.

Elmsley, although perhaps overzealous, was a generous benefactor. He supported the construction of the first Catholic free school in Toronto and presented land for St. Michael's College and St. Basil's Church. In 1848, he and another supporter personally assumed the debt of St. Michael's Cathedral to the tune of $57,600. About the same time, Elmsley began subdividing the Clover Hill property, naming streets after his favourite saints — St. Joseph, St. Mary, St. Alban (now Wellesley), and St. Thomas.

By 1858, Elmsley had moved to Barnstable, just west of the original homestead, where he died in 1863. His heart was enshrined at St. Basil's Church. Charlotte and Remegius occupied Clover Hill again, from 1872 to 1878, while Remegius had a second Barnstable

built on the site of the first. The lot was greatly diminished, to 200 by 650 feet, but the new house was grand — a yellow-brick Gothic structure, with French windows, verandahs, tennis courts, and brick stables. Remegius opened Elmsley Place, a street that ran north from St. Joseph and ended with a semicircular drive in front of Barnstable. He subdivided and sold another twelve lots on that street.

Remegius died in 1910. His wife, Nina, lived at Barnstable until 1921, when the last part of the once-extensive Elmsley estate went to St. Michael's College.

Barnstable was eventually demolished for a new residence at St. Michael's named Elmsley Hall. Clover Hill changed hands a number of times, ending as a boarding house when it was finally expropriated by the city and demolished to make way for new streets. A student residence at St. Michael's was named Cloverhill Hall in deference to the great benefactor's estate.

ELMSLEY VILLA
John Elmsley

John Elmsley built Elmsley Villa, close to modern Bay and Grosvenor Streets, just south of the less impressive Clover Hill, in around 1837. About a mile and a half from York, the property, stretching from present-day College to St. Joseph, and from Yonge to Queen's Park, was a remote location. There are stories of guests getting lost en route to the villa in the thick woods. The gate lodge stood at what is now the corner of Yonge and College Streets.

The house was roughcast over brick and built in the Classical style. Imposing Doric columns, tall shuttered windows, a balcony, and a conservatory added to its aristocratic air. It was surrounded by tall trees on three sides and the grounds were attractively landscaped with winding paths, shady nooks, and a large apple orchard close to the house. Grain fields stretched out beyond the gardens.

The Elmsley property is probably best remembered for an infamous event that took place there long before Clover Hill or Elmsley Villa were built. Versions from the two families involved differ, but most agree that the incident began when John Ridout, working in his brother's office as a law student, went to see Samuel Peters Jarvis about a civil suit against his father, Secretary William Jarvis. The two quarrelled, and Jarvis expelled the hot-tempered youth from his office. Some time later, Ridout attacked Jarvis on the street with a stick, seriously injuring his hand. Jarvis knocked Ridout to the ground, and Ridout challenged him to a duel.

On July 12, 1817, the opponents met behind a barn in a large field on the Elmsley property. John reputedly shot early, on the count of two, but missed his target. Sam was instructed to take his shot, and he hit Ridout in the neck, fatally wounding him. By the time medical aid arrived, Ridout was dead — the last man to be killed in a duel in Toronto. Jarvis was arrested, but was acquitted eventually, according to practice of the day. Some believed that Jarvis's aim had been affected by the injury to his hand and that he hadn't meant to kill his opponent. Others vilified Jarvis for taking his shot when Ridout had no chance, having already discharged his weapon. Jarvis later published his account of the events, but for many Sundays following, Mrs. Ridout would mount the front steps of St. James Cathedral after the service and curse her son's assassin.

John Simcoe Macaulay and his wife, Ann Elmsley, occupied Elmsley Villa for about five years in the early 1840s. By the end of that decade, John Elmsley had moved back to Clover Hill. The house was rented out, at first to Henry Sherwood, Charlotte Elmsley's father. When the capital was once again transferred to Toronto in 1849, after rioting in Montreal over the Rebellion Losses Bill, Elmsley Villa became the official residence of Governor General Lord Elgin and was the centre of many fine entertainments.

Elmsley Villa, at the northwest corner of modern Grosvenor and Bay Streets, during the 1840s. When the property was subdivided in the mid-1850s, the house projected into the proposed road. The resulting easterly jog in Bay Street exists to this day. MTRL JRR T11395

Map of the Township of York, *by John O. Browne (1851).*
Although the Macaulay property to the south was subdivided, the Elmsley Villa estate was largely intact at the time this map was drawn.
Gore Vale, Moss Park, and The Home Wood are identified on the park lots, while the map also locates some of the estates on the Davenport escarpment.

In the mid-1850s, Alexander Clark bought the estate for development. He laid out Granville, Grosvenor, and Breadalbane Streets. The villa projected into the line of St. Vincent Street (later Bay Street), so the street was redirected. The easterly jog in Bay remains to this day. Elmsley Villa became the fourth Knox College, from 1855 to 1875, but the building was demolished to make way for the Central Presbyterian Church, which in turn disappeared during construction of Bay Street in 1923.

CAER HOWELL
William Dummer Powell

William Dummer Powell was born in Boston in 1755, the son of Loyalist John Powell and his wife, Jane Grant, a wealthy heiress. In 1776, William left America for England, where he studied law and was called to the bar at Inner Temple, London. In London, William married Anne Murray. They returned to British North America, first to Montreal, then Niagara, arriving finally at York, where John Graves Simcoe appointed Powell a judge. Upon his arrival, Powell was granted Park lot 12 and additional property in York Township. Park lot 12 ran north from Lot Street, between present University Avenue and McCaul Street.

Powell first erected a rather plain but imposing Georgian house in town. The Royal York Hotel occupies the site today. In 1810, on his park lot, Powell built a large country home south of present-day Orde Street, close to University. He named both his properties Caer Howell for the family seat of his forebears, the Ap Howells of Wales. The country property was Powell's primary residence from 1810 to 1820. The large house faced south to the bay, and a charming stream ran through the property. Powell also had a private burial vault built, surrounded by a brick wall.

Powell, the father of eight children, was a successful lawyer. By 1816, he had become Speaker for the Legislative Council. In that year, his lifelong ambition was realized at last with his appointment as Chief Justice of Upper Canada.

Some of the Powell offspring were extremely headstrong, to their serious detriment. A daughter, Anne, fell in love with John Beverley Robinson, a neighbour who was a brilliant lawyer and a rising member of the city's elite. Robinson married an English lady in 1817, but Anne continued to send him love letters. When the Robinsons set off on a trip to Britain in 1822, Anne broke out of the room where she had been detained, chased the couple to New York, and sailed in pursuit on the next available ship. Sadly, the vessel crashed in the North Sea and Anne was lost.

A son, Jeremiah, involved in trade in the Caribbean, was captured by the Spanish and sentenced to death. For many months, Powell explored every avenue of introduction to the Spanish Court — in America, England, and Spain. His dogged persistence finally succeeded in winning his son's freedom. Another son, William Dummer Jr., eloped to the United States. When he died, his wife and two young girls moved in with the Powells. One of these beloved granddaughters was Mary Boyles Powell, who later married William Botsford Jarvis.

In 1828, Powell sold fifty acres to Bishop Strachan for King's College. In the 1830s, he opened what later became William Street, which ran north from Queen to the private cemetery.

The Powells lived mostly in their Front Street home from 1820 until William died in 1834. After his death, the family began laying out streets on the property and naming them after relations. John Howard surveyed William Street and opened Dummer Street (now St. Patrick) in 1846. Caer Howell Street linked University to McCaul, just south of the burial ground. Murray Street, running north beyond Orde, was severed into large parcels intended for prosperous families.

William Dummer Powell (1755–1834) was Chief Justice of Upper Canada from 1816 to 1825.
This portrait was painted by Grove Sheldon Gilbert in 1834, shortly before Powell's death. MTRL T13769

Proposed additions for Caer Howell, from a pencil drawing done by W. D. Powell some time in the 1830s. The house stood north of modern Queen Street, west of University Avenue.
MTRL JRR T11436

Henry Layton bought Caer Howell in 1837 and turned it into a sports club. It was enlarged in 1853 and again in 1860. This photograph, taken just after the turn of the century, shows Caer Howell in its hotel days, before it was demolished in 1915.
MTRL T10990

Mrs. Powell died in 1949, in her ninety-first year. She was buried with her husband in the vault on the Caer Howell property, but in 1869 the graveyard was deconsecrated and the dead were reinterred at St. James Cemetery.

In 1837, Henry Layton bought the Powells' country home and converted it into an elaborate sports club, with bowling greens and racket courts. Caer Howell later became a hotel and tavern, frequented by high-spirited varsity students. The property degenerated, and the building was demolished in 1915. Mount Sinai Hospital stands on the site today. The only street named by the Powells that remains today is Murray Street, named for Mrs. Powell's family.

The Grange in 1865. Sarah Anne Boulton sits on the porch, while a maid peeks from an upstairs window. As photography was a relatively new invention, all of the family's prized possessions were trotted out for the occasion, including the horses and the lawnmower. MTRL T30716

THE GRANGE
D'Arcy Boulton Jr.

In 1808, D'Arcy Boulton Jr. bought park lot 13 from the estate of Solicitor General Robert Gray for £350. The property ran between modern McCaul and Beverley Streets and the new owner named his estate for the Boulton ancestral home.

D'Arcy Jr., born in England in 1785, was the eldest son of Attorney General D'Arcy Boulton. Although the son articled in his father's law firm, he was never particularly interested in a law career. He eventually went into the dry goods and grocery business and became a successful merchant. His wife, Sarah Ann Robinson, was a sister of John Beverly Robinson and another member of York's elite.

In 1817, Boulton began work on the foundations of his new home, making it one of the four oldest buildings now standing in Toronto. Boulton designed the two-storey brick house himself. A short time later, he added another twenty acres to the Grange estate.

Like other Georgian homes of its day, the Grange was a surprisingly elegant residence, far more sophisticated than one would expect in a backwoods outpost. It was the home of a genteel and aristocratic family, a replica of those estates scattered about the English countryside. Marion McRae and Anthony Adamson wrote about such early Upper Canadian homes in *The Ancestral Roof*: "This was not a shelter for immediate physical needs but a house 'like the one at home,' the simple dignified epitome of centuries of British experience." The balance and grace of the Grange were typical of Georgian design. So, too, were the grand entry with semicircular transom, the centre hall, and the fine interior panelling. McRae and Adamson remind:

> We are looking at fine houses, built for people of taste and some means at the beginning of the nineteenth century. The tractless wilderness might be close at hand, but so was the port of Montreal with its cabinet-makers and silversmiths. To it, under billowing canvas in the tall ships of England and France, came textiles and tea sets, tobacco and spices, fine crystal and dinner wares.

The "tractless wilderness" was indeed just beyond a tiny clearing surrounding the Grange. In the early days, Boulton horses drove off a bear that wandered into the pasture. Mrs. Powell wrote to her brother describing the remote location of the Grange: "Mrs. D'Arcy might as well be in Kingston, the roads cut off all communication with her." In spite of its isolation, this little oasis of civilization came to occupy a position of prominence in the social life of York and later, Toronto. The Boultons and their social circle formed the core of the Family Compact, the province's governing elite.

The carriage drive originally entered past a gatekeeper's lodge on Lot Street, next to the Powells' property. Inside the Grange, a graceful, free-standing stairway dominated the spacious entrance hall and curved up to the second floor. Midway was a large leaded glass rendition of the family crest and motto, *Dux vitae ratio*, "the guide to life is reason." The drawing rooms and dining area were finished in black walnut. Around 1843, the Boultons added a grapery, a two-storey west wing with a library, a Regency-style orangery on the east, and a spacious second-floor music room for large social gatherings. Boulton also had lacrosse and cricket fields and a race-track built on the property.

Boulton had always viewed the Grange estate as an investment to be subdivided and sold off as values rose. The first lots went in 1828; the northern half, fifty-one acres above College, went to King's College to make up the western part of the campus. Sales were somewhat slow from 1832 to 1845, probably because the Garrison Reserve west of the fort was opened to development about the same time, but the racecourse had disappeared by 1850. Some of the grandstand was later incorporated into a greenhouse.

After D'Arcy Boulton Jr. died, Sarah Ann lived on in the house. The eldest surviving son, William Henry, was a lawyer and active politician, later a member of the Legislative Assembly and Mayor of Toronto. William's legal firm amassed liabilities in the tens of

Goldwin Smith in his library at The Grange in 1909. MTRL T32416

thousands of pounds and he was regularly plagued by debts. Just before his marriage to Harriette Mann Dixon, Sarah Ann deeded the Grange and twenty acres to William. He was preparing to sell it off to satisfy creditors when his younger brother intervened and repurchased the property for his mother. Sarah Ann preserved the Grange by willing it instead to Harriette, leaving her daughter-in-law complete discretion to dispose of it as she wished upon her death.

After William died in 1874, Harriette married Professor Goldwin Smith, renowned English essayist, historian, and political commentator. The Smiths began renovations in keeping with the Grange's aristocratic air. They replaced the original wooden portico with the stone one that survives and converted the grapery into a much-used library.

Subdivision continued. Beverley Street was laid out with large and highly fashionable lots in the 1870s. Dundas was put through in 1877 after the last gardens were sold off, but the Goldwin Smiths still enjoyed an idyllic setting. Wrote Smith in his 1910 memoirs:

The Grange at Toronto, with its lawn and its old elms, is the counterpart in style and surroundings of a little English mansion. It is the only specimen of the kind that I happen to have seen on this side of the Atlantic…. In summer, only chimes were wanting to make me fancy that I was in England.

In a letter to Sir Edmund Walker in 1903, Smith wrote, "I have often felt some compunction at having this place, in the midst of a great city, given up to the sole enjoyment of two old people." Harriette died in 1909, her husband the following year. On Walker's fortunate suggestion, Harriette left the Grange to the fledgling Art Museum of Toronto. From 1911 to 1918, the house was used for exhibitions, and then for a number of other administrative functions as the Art Gallery of Ontario grew up around it. During the early 1970s, the building was carefully restored to its original grandeur as a gentleman's house of the late 1830s.

Though the Grange is now tucked away behind the Art Gallery of Ontario, the spacious front lawn and oval carriage drive survive. Neighbouring streets that still bear their Boulton names are Grange Road, D'Arcy Street, and Henry Street.

BROOKFIELD
John Denison

Although the Brookfield estate belongs geographically with properties farther west, John Denison was the head of a large family of Toronto landholders who had several park lot estates in the area between Spadina and Dufferin. Wrote Paul Gagan in *The Denison Family of Toronto*, "For over a century, from 1797 until the death in 1925 of George Denison III, the history of the family and the city were inextricably linked."

Most published histories declare that Simcoe named his new capital for the Duke of York, after his victory against the French in August 1793, but the Denison family maintains a different story. When Simcoe suggested the family settle in the town he intended to name Dublin, John Denison responded that no Yorkshireman would live in a place of that name, and came up with the alternative.

John Denison was born in Headon County, Yorkshire, in 1755. He was a captain of the militia, a miller, and a brewer. In December 1782, he married Sophia Taylor, whose father owned several large estates around Dovercourt, Essex. Sophia was a childhood friend of Elizabeth Russell, so when Peter Russell received his appointment to Upper Canada, the Russells persuaded the Denisons to emigrate.

Denison initially settled at Kingston, starting a partnership with money loaned by Peter Russell.

When the business failed, Russell convinced the Denisons to come to York, where they occupied Castle Frank for a number of years. In 1804, Russell installed his friend on Petersfield as farm manager. Under Denison's management from 1804 to 1807, Petersfield prospered, with potatoes as the main crop. Over the years, Denison received several grants and began to accumulate property, including the park lot immediately west of Petersfield.

Denison also purchased property overlooking the Humber River, which the family named Black Creek Farm. An infant daughter was buried on the farm, and since about 1801, a six-acre parcel — St. John's on the Humber — has been used as a private family cemetery.

In 1815, Denison bought park lot 25 for £200 from the original patentee, surgeon David Burns. He built his mansion, Brookfield House, at the northwest corner of modern Queen and Ossington. Enormous willows cast shadows across the fine lawns and gardens. Although John Denison died in October 1824, his widow lived on at Brookfield for many years.

Because of an error in Denison's will, he failed to make proper provision for two sons and a daughter. As dictated by Upper Canada's laws at the time, all of the property went to the eldest son, George Taylor Denison, with one exception. In 1845, Sophia transferred Brookfield House and four acres surrounding it to John Fennings Taylor, who had married her daughter, Elizabeth. John Taylor was also Sophia's nephew, being her brother's son. Sophia died in 1852 and was buried at St. John's Cemetery with her husband.

After the Lunatic Asylum was constructed on the south side of Queen in 1846, the area around Brookfield House deteriorated. The house was demolished, and smallish lots were sold. Ossington Avenue received its name from the family seat of Ossington House in Nottinghamshire. Brookfield Street was opened, as were Fennings and Rolyat (Taylor spelled backwards), both named for the Denisons' son-in-law.

Captain John Denison (1755–1824). The Captain's Brookfield, on park lot 25, was the first of many Denison estates on Queen Street between Spadina and Dufferin. MTRL JRR T15101

BELLEVUE
George Taylor Denison

John Denison's eldest son was born in England in 1783 and arrived at York as a young man with his parents and two other brothers in 1796. George Taylor Denison inherited the bulk of the family property, but he also added to his landholdings throughout his lifetime. Much of the property he acquired through his four marriages.

In December 1806, George married Esther Borden Lippincott, the only child of Captain Richard Lippincott, a wealthy United Empire Loyalist who owned three thousand acres in the Richmond Hill area.

George Denison, like many Denisons who followed him, was a military man and a strong believer in the superiority of the British Empire. He served with the militia in 1812, beginning a lifelong affiliation with Upper Canada's military. One of his tasks during the war was to cut a strategically important route from the Garrison to Lambton Mills — today's Dundas Street.

In 1815, George purchased park lot 17 and the eastern half of park lot 18, 156 acres in total, from Elizabeth Russell at £5 per acre. The property actually adjoined Petersfield, where his father had arrived little more than a decade earlier. George's estate was bounded by present Queen, Lippincott, Bloor, and Augusta.

In the same year, Denison started his grand home, Bellevue, at the northeast corner of modern Denison Avenue and Denison Square. The property contained a large farm, complete with an orchard, and there was a ravine to the north. The house, half a mile north of Lot Street, was situated in heavy

woods, and George cleared only enough trees to let in sufficient light. The solid Georgian home stood at the head of a long carriage drive (now Denison Avenue) overhung by branches. Edward Chadwick made the following observations in *Ontarian Families* in 1894:

> The house is remarkable as being built with four sides, facing due north, south, east and west, the only house in Toronto so built, except perhaps one other, the old Hospital on the corner of King and John Streets, not now in existence.

Esther and George had four children: Richard Lippincott, who went on to build Dover Court; George Taylor II, owner of Rusholme; Mary Elizabeth, who married John Fennings Taylor; and Robert Brittain. Esther died in 1823. In 1827, George married his cousin, Maria Taylor, who died a short four years later. His third wife, Elizabeth Caldwell Todd, died in 1849. A fourth, Maria Priscilla Coates, survived her husband, dying in 1887.

From 1822 to 1837, Denison organized and led a voluntary cavalry troop, mostly at his own expense, and he commanded this regiment during the Rebellion of 1837. The troop later became the Governor General's Body Guard (now the Governor General's Horse Guard), the first eight commanding officers of which were Denisons. In 1846, George took command of the 4th Battalion of Toronto militia. He held this post until his death.

In the last year of his life, Denison had the southern part of the Bellevue estate surveyed. At the time of his death in 1853, he was one of wealthiest people in Upper Canada. His will was reported to be the

This portrait of George Taylor Denison I (1783–1853) was painted some time in the 1840s. His will, the largest probated in Ontario at the time of his death, included title to 556 acres in present-day Toronto. MTRL T31333

Bellevue, the home of George Taylor Denison I, in 1865. By this time, the house was occupied by a son, Robert, and most of the estate had been subdivided into Bellevue and Denison Avenues and Esther, Borden, Lippincott, Major, and Robert Streets. Archives of Ontario ACC 1582 S. 1305

largest ever probated in Ontario to that date, and it included title to 556 acres in Toronto.

Robert, the third son, inherited Bellevue, although some of the property had already been severed and sold. He, too, was a military man, and rose to the rank of colonel with the Queen's Own Rifles. Most of the Bellevue estate was subdivided during his tenure in the 1850s.

Robert donated property and building funds for St. Stephen's-in-the-Fields, just north of Bellevue, south of College. Perhaps it was divine intervention that saved him the night an intruder broke into the house. Grabbing a sword that hung above his bed, Colonel Denison confronted the assailant, who fired a shot and then fled through a broken window. Robert later discovered a hole in his

nightshirt and a bullet lodged in the clock behind him.

Robert Denison sold the house in 1889, and it was demolished in 1890. By 1894, the area that had once been the Bellevue estate was a heavily populated district. It underwent further change between 1900 and 1914, as eastern and northern European immigrants arrived and Kensington Market sprang up.

Denison street names abound in the area — Denison Square, Denison Avenue, Bellevue Avenue, and Major, Robert, Borden, and Lippincott Streets. Some others have since disappeared. Augusta replaced Esther Street, Bellevue Place is now Denison Square, and St. Patrick Street — which George named in honour of his Irish third wife, Eleanor — is now Dundas.

Crookshank's residence before 1865 (from a drawing by Stephen Heward). The home stood on a large estate west of modern Bathurst Street.
One of the first homes in that district, it was used by the Americans as a headquarters when York fell during the War of 1812. MTRL JRR T11184

CROOKSHANK ESTATE
George Crookshank

George Crookshank was born in New York City in 1773. His father was owner and captain of a trading vessel and immigrated to New Brunswick after the American Revolution. George first went to work aboard his uncle's merchant ships trading to Jamaica. A sister, Catherine Crookshank, married John McGill, who was appointed commissary of stores and provisions at York in 1792. George and another sister, Rachel, followed Mrs. McGill to York in December 1796.

George was awarded the position of commissariat in charge of supplies for Fort York and other garrisons in the area. The Simcoes held both George and Rachel in high regard, and this may explain George's rapid advancement. A series of promotions followed: Assistant Commissary General in 1814, Receiver General in 1819, Legislative Councillor from 1821 until 1841, and Director of the Bank of Upper Canada from 1822 to 1827.

As a United Empire Loyalist, George received a grant of twelve hundred acres on his arrival in Upper Canada. He built a town house on Peter Street, which was at the western edge of town at that time, but he also acquired the western half of park lot 18 as well as lots 19 and 20. He constructed a large farm home halfway between Lot Street and the second concession (Bloor Street). He then built Crookshank's Lane along the eastern border of his land to connect the estate to town. (This semi-private roadway eventually became Bathurst Street.) The Crookshank house was one of the few buildings in that section of York Township prior to 1812, and when York fell to the Americans during the war, the home was looted and commandeered by the Americans for headquarters.

In 1821, at forty-eight years of age, George married Sarah Lambert of New York and acquired property in the United States through his wife's family. The Crookshanks had one daughter and two sons and enjoyed a privileged life on their country estate outside York. A staff of eight servants kept the household running smoothly. The residence was later enlarged.

By 1850, Crookshank's health was failing and the city was starting to encroach. The following year, he sold the property to developers, who opened up streets and disposed of large blocks through speculators. The closing sale of Crookshank Estate lots was held in June 1855. Only two years later, some of the parcels were further divided into small lots for working-class buyers. An economic crash followed and the area very slowly developed into Seaton Village.

The Honourable George Crookshank died in 1859. When his will was probated it was valued at £40,986, excluding real estate. Through a period of economic turbulence, George Crookshank had made a considerable fortune.

In 1864, Philip Brown purchased the house, had it moved a hundred yards east, and renovated the building. Nothing remains of the estate today. Even Crookshank's Lane was renamed shortly after George's death; it took on the name of its southern extension — Bathurst Street — in 1870.

The Honourable George Crookshank (1773–1859).
From an oil painting done by Thomas Wood in 1855. MTRL T13681

Sir Casimir Gzowski's home, The Hall, around 1901. Radio personality Peter Gzowski is a great-great-grandson. AO ACC 2039 S2903

THE HALL
Casimir Gzowski

One of the early purchasers of a Crookshank Estate lot was Casimir Gzowski. His seven-acre property was at the southeast corner of modern Bathurst and Dundas Streets.

In *Toronto: 100 Years of Grandeur*, Lucy Both Martyn described Casimir Gzowski as "the most romantic figure in nineteenth century Toronto." Born in 1813, Casimir Stanislaus Gzowski was the son of a Polish count. He was an activist while studying at the University of Poland at Warsaw, and for his part in the Polish revolt of 1832, the Czar's troops pursued Gzowski as he made his escape to Austria.

When the young émigré arrived in the United States in 1834, his English was too poor to practise civil engineering, for which he had trained. Instead, he studied English and law while teaching fencing, violin, and languages at a private school in New England. After obtaining a job as an engineer during the construction of the New York and Erie Railway, Casimir was sent to Canada. There he encountered Lord Sydenham, who, recalling the Gzowskis' kindness during a visit to St. Petersburg, secured the young man an engineering contract to improve Yonge Street. A series of engineering successes followed, and in 1853, with partner David Macpherson, Gzowski made his fortune building the Grand Trunk Railway. He went on to occupy a number of industrial and financial directorships, though perhaps he is best remembered for his work on the International Bridge linking Fort Erie and Buffalo.

In 1858, Gzowski had architect Frederick Cumberland draw up the plans for a Victorian Gothic mansion for his new lot on the western edge of Toronto. The buff-coloured brick house that faced west to Bathurst was surrounded by well-kept lawns, a deer park, a bowling green, and an enclosure for pheasants and exotic birds. Amid the large flower gardens were marble statues and pergolas, and a canon. Casimir was a lover of flowers and tending his exquisite rose garden was a favourite pastime.

Inside the house were spacious halls, opulent receiving rooms, and ornate furnishings. A large corps of footmen, butlers, and maids supported this grand lifestyle reminiscent of the Gzowski family's illustrious past in the courts of Europe.

The Gzowskis were at the centre of social life in Toronto. There were lawn parties, balls, musical soirées, and lavish dinners in the five-hundred-square-foot dining room. As president of numerous sporting and professional associations, Casimir entertained royalty, professional men, and prominent personalities of the age. Two of his daughters danced with the Prince of Wales — later Edward VII — when the young royal visited the city in 1860. A newspaper account in June 1881 describes a visit to The Hall during an evangelical conference in Toronto:

From four to six o'clock of the same day, Sir Casimir Gzowski gave a garden party to which all the delegates to the convention and their friends were invited. Nearly one thousand persons were present.... First came the porter or some other big officer who had a platter of silver on which was placed the small card of introduction — we retaining the larger one. He took the card, read out the names in a very loud voice and we were personally conducted to the Colonel and his wife, who shook hands with everyone. After this, we had access to the eight rooms of the house and grounds.

There were tables laden with all kinds of delicacies to tempt the appetite. Servants, dressed in black broadcloth with swallow tail coats, white vests and white ties, invited us to the spread and every attention was paid to the wants of all.

Gzowski was a generous philanthropist and a moving force behind many institutions of the late 1800s, including The Toronto Stock Exchange, Ontario Jockey Club, Dominion Rifle Association, and the University of Toronto Senate. He was also a warden of St. James Cathedral for many years. For his engineering accomplishments and philanthropic work, Gzowski was knighted in 1890.

By 1884, much of the area around The Hall had been built up. Sir Casimir died in 1898 at eighty-five years of age. Lady Gzowski continued living at The Hall with her married son, Casimir. In 1904, the son sold the property, a portion going to the city for a park. The house was demolished and the site became Alexandra Park, complete with tennis and lawn bowling greens and, appropriately, a rose garden.

The drawing room at The Hall in 1896.
The Bathurst and Dundas residence was already surrounded by development by this time. MTRL T11260

Duncan Cameron's Gore Vale, on the north side of Queen Street, west of what would become Gorevale Avenue.
This photograph was taken between 1900 and 1909, likely after Trinity College purchased the house. The house was later used as a student residence. MTRL T11158

GORE VALE
Duncan Cameron

Park lot 22 was originally granted to Captain Samuel Smith of the Queen's Rangers in 1806. Because it was so far from town, Smith sold the property around 1815 without ever having built a house. He did, however, provide the property with a name. Gore Vale was named after Francis Gore, Lieutenant-Governor from 1806 to 1817. Duncan Cameron purchased the lot from the intervening owner, Charles Shaw, in 1819.

Duncan Cameron was born in Scotland and arrived in York prior to 1801. He was a merchant by trade and an active member of the militia. He commanded the York Volunteers at Queenston Heights in 1812. Five years later, Cameron was appointed to succeed Secretary Jarvis as Registrar, and was made a member of the Legislative Council in 1820. As an influential member of the governing Family Compact, Duncan was viewed unfavourably by reformers like Dr. William Warren Baldwin, who wrote, "Mr. D. Cameron a bird of ill omen is again flapping about the Govt House … the old bird lime is still adhesive to the branches of the Administration."

Cameron built his house in 1817, close to the east lot line at Gore Vale. His unmarried sister, Janet, lived there with him. Gore Vale was a substantial red-brick, three-storey house. Its mansard roof was highly unusual among houses of York at that time. Three dormers graced the roofline, offering the Camerons a lovely view to the lake from their estate. Just west of the house, a tributary of Garrison Creek flowed through a ravine on its way down to the fort.

Cameron died in 1838 without having married and left Gore Vale to his sister. Eleven years later, the Baldwin Reform Government legislated that King's College, formerly affiliated with the Church of England, become the secular University of Toronto. Determined to provide an alternative along strong Anglican lines, Bishop Strachan obtained a royal charter and bought twenty acres from Janet Cameron. In 1851, a Tudor Gothic building was erected on Queen Street, just slightly south and west of Gore Vale, to house Trinity College.

Janet Cameron died in 1853. Henry John, D'Arcy Boulton Jr.'s younger brother, purchased the house and remaining eighty acres. He presented Gore Vale as a wedding gift to his second daughter, Sophia, and her husband, Colonel James Forlong. Forlong died at the estate in 1859. Sophia stayed in the house until 1867, and it remained in the Boulton family for another three years.

The subsequent owner was Edward Oscar Bickford, a wealthy railway contractor who bought the house and surrounding fifty-four acres. He opened two streets running north from Dundas on either side of the house and named them after his daughters, Grace and Beatrice. Bickford died in 1891. That same year, Gore Vale Avenue was opened.

In 1904, Trinity College purchased the remaining Gore Vale estate. The house was used for a variety of purposes. For a time it housed the Keeley Institute for alcohol rehabilitation, and it was also a student residence. The city bought the grounds in 1912, and from 1915 to 1920, the house served as a hospital. Six years after the hospital vacated the building, the dilapidated and vandalized ruin that had once been Gore Vale was demolished.

Aeneas Shaw's Oak Hill, north of modern Queen Street, east of Shaw.
The log house on the left was built in 1794. The building on the right was erected in 1798 and was the first frame house in the York area. MTRL JRR T11498

OAK HILL
Aeneas Shaw

Aeneas Shaw, born in Strathcairn, Scotland, descended from the Shaw clan of Tordarroch. Born about 1740, he arrived in New York around 1770 and entered the army as an ensign. He distinguished himself as an able British soldier during the American Revolution and was promoted to Captain with the Queen's Rangers. After the British surrender, Shaw's property in Long Island was confiscated and he was obliged to leave America. He led his contingent of Rangers on snowshoe through the dead of winter via New Brunswick to Montreal. For this feat, he earned the attention of John Graves Simcoe, who later praised Shaw as a man of "Education, Ability & Loyalty ... one of those Gentlemen who is most likely to effect a permanent Landed Establishment in this Country."

Shaw arrived in York in 1793 and he led the detachment that cleared York and built the first garrison. His was one of the first families to settle at the new capital as well, and their first home was a log house beside Garrison Creek. When the garrison expanded, his original house became the Commandant's office.

As part of the thousands of acres granted to him as a Loyalist, Shaw received three parcels to the north of York Garrison, totalling five hundred acres. One of these was park lot 23. He settled his family there in 1794, naming the property Oak Hill — a translation of the Gaelic *tordarroch*. That same year, Shaw was appointed to the Legislative Council. As one of the few councillors who attended regularly, he was valued by Simcoe and considered indispensable by Russell. Shaw's decisiveness and energy earned him later appointments to the Executive Council and a number of other public offices.

The Shaw land was heavily wooded, with pine, oak, hickory, and beech. The house stood half a mile north of today's Queen Street, just north of the stream that flowed down to the garrison. This pioneer log house stood until about 1875, but in 1798, having had seven sons and six daughters with his first wife, Anne Gosline, Shaw required a much roomier residence. That year he built what some people in York considered a somewhat pretentious larger home. Standing slightly east of the original homestead, near present Harrison and Crawford Streets, it was the first frame residence in the York area. Queen Victoria's father, the Duke of Kent, stayed here when he visited York as a young officer in 1802.

The area around Oak Hill was wilderness for many years; in 1806, there were still only three homes in the area. Anne died that year, and Shaw married Margaret Hickman shortly afterward.

After attaining the rank of Lieutenant Colonel and already in late middle age, in 1803 Shaw was retired on half pay and made an honorary councillor. But, as war approached, he was gazetted Major-General and placed in charge of training the militia. It was Shaw who led the militia in an unsuccessful defence of the town in April 1813. The War was tragic for the family in another way. Shaw's daughter Sophia was engaged to General Isaac Brock, who fell in the Battle of Queenston Heights.

As a United Empire Loyalist, Shaw had been granted six thousand acres, with an additional twelve hundred acres each for every family member. Most of this land he left unimproved, and in 1803 he began selling off lots. The five hundred acres around York he retained until his death in 1814. A son, Charles Shaw, took over Oak Hill.

Captain Alexander Shaw, a grandson of Aeneas, was still living in the house in 1871, and the property was largely intact until he began selling off portions in the 1870s. The southern corner, west of Crawford, was subdivided first.

Today, a provincial historical plaque on Queen Street West, opposite Strachan Avenue, at the entrance to Trinity Bellwoods Park, commemorates "Major-General The Honourable Aeneas Shaw". Shaw Street serves as a reminder of Aeneas Shaw's Oak Hill, as it marks the western lot line.

Dover Court in the 1890s. Richard Lippincott Denison's house stood at the head of what is now Lakeview Avenue, west of Ossington Avenue. The estate, part of Captain John Denison's Brookfield property, was named for Sophia Taylor Denison's family home in Essex. MTRL JRR T11196

DOVER COURT
Richard Lippincott Denison

Dover Court, northwest of Dundas and Ossington, was built by Richard Lippincott Denison, eldest son of George Taylor Denison and Esther Borden Lippincott. Richard Lippincott was born in 1814 and raised at Bellevue, about a mile east of what eventually became his own estate. He became a farmer and businessman, and, in true Denison fashion, was very involved in the provincial militia.

Part of park lots 25 and 26 came to Richard through his father's inheritance. In 1837, Richard married Susan Hepbourne and built their first home north and slightly east of his late grandfather's Brookfield House. He named the property for his grandmother's ancestral home in Essex. The first house was surrounded by lawn and orchards, with a kitchen garden in front. Farm fields ran from behind the house up to modern Bloor Street.

In 1853, the Denisons built a much larger and more elegant home on a slight rise in the centre of the property. This second home was red brick, and a high gable crowned the second storey. Wide verandahs graced the front of the house and the west face. By this time, with George Taylor Denison II installed next door at Rusholme, the part of Dundas that ran northwest from Ossington was known as Denison's Terrace.

An Anglican chapel was built in the gardens in 1857 for the family and tenant farmers. This was the forerunner to St. Anne's Church, founded in 1862 and demolished about thirty years later. Richard also had a substantial road built straight up from Dundas, and the boulevards were planted with trees. Today's Lakeview Avenue is still uncharacteristically wide, a reminder of its earlier days as a carriage drive. A Denison family history gives the account of a lumber wagon driver who persisted in taking a shortcut along Dover Court's carriage drive. Colonel Denison pulled the man off his wagon, whipped him, and sent the horses ahead. The driver never repeated his transgression.

Richard succeeded his father as Commander of the Governor General's Body Guard. He was Lieutenant Colonel with the 4th Battalion of Sedentary Militia, and Commanding Officer of the West Toronto Reserve Militia. He was also renowned for breeding exceptional cavalry mounts.

Colonel Denison died in 1878, survived by his wife, eight sons, one daughter, and a stepdaughter. He reserved Dover Court and a surrounding lot at the top of Lakeview Avenue for his wife's use during her lifetime, with a stipulation that the name be retained. He was an old-style English patriarch and had always hoped that a son would buy the family homestead. He willed lots along Dovercourt Road to each of his children and ordered the remainder sold.

Susan died in 1889. Richard Lippincott II lived at Dover Court for a while. Richard, like his uncle, Robert, was also awakened one night by noises in his house. With sword in hand, he threw open the cellar door and wildly slashed at a ghostly figure. Feathers flew everywhere from the down bedding that had been hung out to air. There was no intruder.

Dover Court was altered and sold in 1894. It was eventually demolished in 1933 for two new homes. Lakeview Avenue remains, as do Hepbourne Street and Dovercourt Road.

RUSHOLME
George Taylor Denison II

George Taylor Denison II, born in 1816, was the second son of George Taylor Denison of Bellevue. After attending Upper Canada College, he studied law and became a prominent lawyer, although he retired from practice in 1856 to become an entrepreneur. George also succeeded his father and brother in command of the Governor General's Body Guard. Through the years, he rubbed elbows with an international elite that included princes, governors general, and ministers.

At twenty-one years of age, George was made a lieutenant with the Queen's Light Dragoons, and he moved up through the ranks to lieutenant colonel by 1853. In 1860, after commanding the First Regiment of the York Light Dragoons, he was made a full colonel. In addition to his interest in matters military, according to Paul Gagan in *The Denison Family of Toronto*, he also "retained his grandfather's attachment to the soil, lavishing care and time on the fields and orchards of Rusholme which became a model of productive, scientific farming."

In 1838, George Denison II married Mary Anne Dewson, and the following year he built his home on the part of park lot 27 given to him by his father. He named it after the park-like property of a Manchester relative, Joseph Denison. White gates and a gabled gatekeeper's cottage marked the entrance to the curving carriage drive from the corner of modern Dundas and Rusholme Streets.

George's division of his family's landholdings had a major influence on the development of west Toronto. The Denisons lived the life of country squires, with their mansions protected by forests and fields, even as they subdivided nearby land and reaped sizeable profits. During the 1850s, as property values rose and park lot property could command as much as £200 an acre, George II sold some of the land north of Dundas.

Rusholme was at the centre of a cosmopolitan social life. The house was the scene of elaborate soirées and balls, and the daughters were presented at court. As a Confederate sympathizer, George was visited at Rusholme by General Robert E. Lee. He was also visited by a number of other royal and military personalities. Mary Anne's brother, George Dewson, was actually a colonel in the Confederate Army. The house was filled with military trophies and family portraits. On special occasions, the Denison coach — emblazoned with the family crest and attended by liveried coachmen — would sweep out the drive.

George Taylor Denison II died in 1873. The house went to his widow, but already two-thirds of the property had been sold off. Rusholme Road was subdivided in 1883 and, by 1884, the property surrounding the house had been reduced to a square bounded by Dovercourt Road, St. Anne's Road, Rusholme Street, and College Street.

Although George and his wife had seven sons, the second son, Frederick, inherited the house. The eldest son, George Taylor Denison III, was already living in his own home at Heydon Villa by that time. Frederick added a ballroom and a library at Rusholme. The twenty-one rooms were eventually filled with his eight children.

Frederick Denison followed in the military tradition of the Denison family. He was famous for an unusual expedition in 1884. With a group of Canadian voyageurs, he accompanied the Wolseley expedition up the Nile to rescue General Charles Gordon, who was under siege at Khartoum. After a gruelling ordeal, the unlikely group discovered that Khartoum had fallen and that Gordon had been beheaded.

Frederick's wife stayed on at Rusholme after his death in 1896. Interestingly, Rusholme was one of the last homes in Toronto to convert to electricity; it had gas lighting long into the electric age. When his son inherited the property, the house was run down. Increasing taxes and the cost of maintaining household staff had contributed to its deterioration. After he died in 1953, his widow sold the property, and the house was demolished to make way for apartments.

Rusholme in 1895, while it was occupied by Frederick Charles Denison, the son of George Taylor II.
Frederick was part of the ill-starred expedition to rescue General Gordon at Khartoum in 1884–85. MTRL T11194

Rusholme was home to a dynasty. For 115 years it had been occupied by a single family noted for its involvement in the development of the city. Its men had seen service in every war in which Canada had played a part. The following street names preserve the neighbourhood's Denison roots: Rusholme Park Crescent, Rusholme Road, Rusholme Drive, and Dewson Street.

HEYDON VILLA
George Taylor Denison III

George Taylor Denison III was born at Bellevue in 1839, just before his parents moved to their new estate, Rusholme. At sixteen, he joined the cavalry corps his grandfather had organized and was quickly promoted to Captain. His rise through the militia was indeed rapid. In 1866, he commanded the troop as Lieutenant Colonel at Niagara during the Fenian Raids. He also saw action as a commander in 1885 during the Northwest Rebellion. In civilian life, Denison studied law and became a barrister.

In 1864, George married Caroline Macklem. That same year he began building perhaps the largest and most grand of all the Denison homes — Heydon Villa. The name came from his great-grandfather's birthplace, Headon, Yorkshire, and the house was situated northeast of his father's home, on a hill west of today's Dovercourt Road, just south of College.

The red-brick mansion had a distinctly southern style, with a wide verandah supported by Doric columns, a Grecian pedimented entry, shuttered windows, and eighteen-foot ceilings. Above the entry to the twenty-five-by-thirty-five-foot dining room hung a bison head. Almost twice that size, the drawing room featured ornate plaster mouldings, imported marble fireplaces, and gilt-framed mirrors. At this fine home, Colonel Denison also compiled an impressive two-thousand-volume library and collected weapons from around the world.

South of the house were gardens — a sylvan retreat with rustic bridges, wild strawberries, and trilliums. The grounds closer to the house were more formally landscaped with rose gardens.

Like his father, and following the ideals of his uncle — Colonel George Dewson of the Confederate Army — George also sympathized with the South during the American Civil War. His home became a gathering place for Confederate sympathizers, and agents smuggled documents to this safe haven. When the *Georgian*, a Great Lakes raider, was seized by the Union, George was persuaded to purchase the ship to secure its release. A lengthy political battle ensued.

Following the *Georgian* incident, a bitter and insolvent George wrote a "History of Cavalry" and submitted his manuscript in a Russian competition. He won a prize of five thousand rubles from the Czar and quite a bit of attention at home. In 1877, the Premier of Ontario offered George the position of Police Magistrate of Toronto. The appointment surprised Denison. In his memoirs, he wrote, "I had made no request for any appointment, and had no desire to take a public office. In fact it was contradictory to the tradition of my family, no one of whom up to that time had ever taken any civil appointment."

As Police Magistrate, Colonel Denison tried most crimes except those requiring a jury, such as murder and high treason. Up until 1917, he heard ninety percent of the indictable offences in Toronto. He wrote, "I doubt if there is any

George Taylor Denison II's sons circa 1877. From left to right are Frederick Charles (who inherited Rusholme), Henry Tyrwhitt, George Taylor III (of Heydon Villa), Septimus Julius Augustus (indeed, the seventh son), John, Egerton Edmund Augustus, and Clarence Alfred Kinsey Denison. MTRL T10120

*Heydon Villa from the garden. Rudyard Kipling was one of many guests
who enjoyed lavish entertainments at the College and Dovercourt estate.* AO ACC 1582 S.1310

judge or magistrate, either in Canada or in England, who has tried as many indictable offences as I have in the last forty years."

Heydon Villa was the site of many fine dinners and gatherings; notable guests included Rudyard Kipling and British politician Joseph Chamberlain. In February 1885, Caroline, mother of six, died. It was just after this loss that George was dispatched to the Northwest with his command. He was remarried in 1887 to Helen Amanda Mair.

The city was close by, but still removed from Heydon Villa, and Colonel Denison was able to walk to city hall each day. During the fire of 1904, the whole family congregated on the widow's walk and watched with concern as the downtown burned.

George Taylor Denison III died in 1925. He had been President of the Royal Society and the Canadian Military Institute, and an ever-active member of the British Empire League. The house was vacant until it was demolished four years later. Heydon Park Road was cut through the property, and Heydon Terrace Apartments were erected nearby on Dovercourt Road. In 1965, the armoury built on Dufferin was named Denison Armoury in honour of George Denison III.

Colonel Denison's death marked the end of an era. The large Denison properties had been subdivided, most of the homes demolished, and the real estate fortunes diluted. George's brother Septimus Julius Denison is quoted in *Forgotten Canadians*:

> At the time of grandfather's [the first George Taylor] death … he left … a goodly fortune; but as he had eight children survive him, as my father had nine and as in Canada properties are usually divided equally, it is not difficult to understand that, if I had any ability at all, it would be a greater asset to help me in my career than my inheritance of a seventy-second part of my grandfather's estate.

THE GEORGE PLAYTER PROPERTIES

Captain George Playter was born in Surrey, England, in February 1736. He later immigrated to New Jersey, where he married Elizabeth Welding, a Quaker, in 1765, and joined the Society of Friends. George and Elizabeth went on to have five sons and five daughters.

The Playters owned a great deal of land in the Philadelphia area, but when the American Revolution began, George sided with the British. Henry Scadding presented Playter's account in *Toronto of Old*:

> He used to give a somewhat humorous account of his sudden return to the military creed of ordinary mundane men. "Lie there, Quaker!!" cried he to his cutaway, buttonless, formal coat as he stripped it off and flung it down for the purpose of donning the soldier's habiliments.

Playter managed to rescue valuable papers and deliver them to the British government; for this he was granted the rank of Captain.

As a result of the Revolutionary War, the Playters lost their Pennsylvania properties and joined the flood of Loyalists to Upper Canada. George arrived at York by way of Kingston in 1796, with at least three sons: John, Eli, and George. That year, Captain Playter was granted park lot 8, the one-hundred-acre strip immediately east of Yonge Street, as well as a two-hundred-acre farm lot that ran east from Yonge along the north side of present-day Bloor Street. The sons also received two-hundred-acre lots. John's lot 17, in the second concession, later became Moore Park. Another son, James, received the lot north of today's Danforth Avenue, and Eli the adjoining property.

Playter's gatehouse stood at what is now the intersection of Parliament and Bloor Streets. It was later used as a studio by Francis Cayley of Drumsnab, but was demolished during construction of the Prince Edward Viaduct during the First World War.

Painting by Owen Staples, 1914. MTRL JRR T11434

A copy of the earliest land grants in the Home District of York, showing landholders, circa 1800.

On June 17, 1790, Captain Playter executed the first property transfer in York Township, selling the southern forty acres of his park lot to John McGill for roughly £56. Playter preferred his farm lot just west of the Don River. He built a house there from which he was able to look across the river to his son's home on the east bank.

George Playter was popular with his neighbours and was known for his animated and jocular temperament. He and his wife made a striking picture as they walked to church in their finery — he in a three-cornered hat, white stockings, and silver knee buckles, and sporting a gold-topped cane, and she in a scoop bonnet and fine shawl.

The Playters were responsible for the first bridge across the Don River. Elizabeth Simcoe described it in her diary entry of June 6, 1796:

> I passed Playter's picturesque bridge over the Donn, it is a butternut Tree fallen across the river the branches still growing in full leaf. Mrs. Playter being timorous, a pole was fastened thro the branches to hold by. Having attempted to pass it, I was determined to proceed but was frightened before I got half way.

The men of the family held a number of public offices. George was appointed Assessor in 1797. His son George was Deputy Sheriff for the Home District, while Eli, James, and John held important civil positions in later years.

The Playter house stood close to today's Castle Frank Road, and the gate lodge stood at the top of modern Parliament Street. A little community of roughly fifty people that sprang up at the southwest corner of the property was called Playterville for a number of years. George added to the property by purchasing a portion of the Castle Frank estate, and on that section he set aside a family burial ground.

In 1822, George Playter passed away. Before his death, he disposed of the remaining portion of park lot 8, on Yonge Street, selling it to Captain John Elmsley. By 1842, most of the Yonge Street property had been subdivided.

George Playter was interred in his private plot at Castle Frank, where Rosedale Heights Secondary School now stands. In 1821, John Small bought the western section of the Playter property, which he later sold to William Botsford Jarvis. In 1834, Francis Cayley bought the eastern side of the Playter property including the old house. There he built his estate, Drumsnab. Although no trace of George Playter's early ownership exists today along Yonge Street or in Rosedale, the family influence is still apparent east of the Don River, where you will find Playter Estates, Playter Boulevard, and Playter Crescent.

McGill Cottage during the 1850s. As stipulated in his uncle's will, Peter McCutcheon changed his name to McGill in order to inherit the property. The site is now occupied by the Metropolitan United Church. Painting by W. Bartram. MTRL T30581

MCGILL COTTAGE
Captain John McGill

John McGill was born in Auckland, Scotland, but he came to North America to serve under Simcoe with the Queen's Rangers during the American Revolution. Afterward, he settled in New Brunswick, and there married Catherine Crookshank, sister of George Crookshank. The McGills moved to Upper Canada in 1792 and John was put in charge of supplying the army. By 1799, as Commissary General of Upper Canada, he had received a number of land grants, including a town lot and park lot 7. McGill preferred to live on his suburban estate, so he had his home — McGill Cottage — built there in 1803, paying the carpenters with land that he owned in Scarborough. McGill Cottage faced down to Lot Street, between present-day Bond and Mutual Streets. During his tenure there, John also served as Receiver General from 1813 to 1819.

McGill's lot was east of the Playter park lot. "Situated in fields at the southern extremity of a stretch of forest, the comfortable and pleasantly-situated residence erected for him for many years seemed a place of abode quite remote from town," wrote Henry Scadding in *Toronto of Old*.

The house was a spacious one-and-a-half-storey Regency cottage with an attractive centre gable and a broad verandah. The prettily treed grounds surrounding the house later came to be known as McGill Square. The remaining southern part of the property was a working farm. Behind the house, woods stretched up to modern Bloor Street. Hunting parties frequently ventured into McGill's bush in search of deer, snipe, and other small game.

Catherine and John had only one child, who died in infancy. Catherine died in 1819. Without an heir, McGill drafted an interesting will. His nephew, Peter McCutcheon, of Montreal, was to inherit the entire property on the condition that he change his surname to McGill. John died in 1834.

Peter McGill began selling off portions of the property in 1836 in one of the earliest subdivisions around York. Church Street, named for St. James Church, was finally extended north of Queen. The segment next to Lot Street was one of the first subdivisions in the city to include laneways flanked by dense row housing. Slightly north, larger lots were subdivided between 1840 and 1842, and Shuter, Crookshank, Gould, and Gerard Streets were opened up. All four Streets were named for McGill connections: Gould for Nathaniel Gould, an officer of the British American Land Company and a friend of the captain; Shuter for Gould's co-director, John Shuter; Gerard for a family friend; and Crookshank for Catherine's relatives. Mutual Street was surveyed by John Howard as a shared road between the McGill property and the Jarvis estate. McGill Street, which bisects the old property, came much later and was actually named for Ann McGill, wife of Bishop Strachan, rather than for Captain McGill.

Most of the homes erected during the 1850s were middle-class houses built on speculation. An exception was architect William Thomas' Oakham House, which he built in 1848 on land purchased from the McGill estate. McGill Cottage was suddenly at the centre of a genteel suburb.

Although much of the northern section was intact into the 1850s, a large block was purchased by the Province in 1850 for a normal school. Under the direction of Egerton Ryerson, it was Ontario's first training institution for elementary school teachers, and the site is now part of Ryerson Polytechnic University.

Peter McGill died in Montreal in 1860, but his brother lived at McGill Cottage until 1870. In that year, McGill Cottage and the two acres surrounding the house were purchased by the Wesleyan Methodists. Here they built Metropolitan Church, now Metropolitan United.

KEARNSEY HOUSE
William Proudfoot / Donald MacKay

William Proudfoot, of Kearnsey House, was an enigmatic character. He occupied a position of prominence in Toronto in the middle of the last century and owned a large estate where he held lavish entertainments. And yet, his year of birth and date and place of death are unknown.

William Proudfoot was likely born around 1800, most probably in Scotland. He arrived in York in about 1816 and nothing more is known about his antecedents. He started as a partner with D'Arcy Boulton Jr. in a dry goods and grocery business. By 1825, Proudfoot had his own successful wholesale and retail venture, selling groceries, bulk goods, and wines. He retired from that venture in the 1830s and married Caroline Brooks Stow in May 1833. Over the years, William purchased a great deal of land in Upper Canada; by 1858 he claimed ownership of seventy thousand acres.

In 1834, Proudfoot was appointed Governor of the British American Assurance Company. When William Allan of Moss Park resigned as first president of The Bank of Upper Canada over political attacks and director apathy, Proudfoot was elected as his successor. Wrote Allan in a letter, "Mr. Proudfoot was not elected from the idea of his being by any means either equal to it or the best they could get. He was the only who was a candidate for it...." The person with real influence throughout Proudfoot's lacklustre presidency was Thomas Gibbs Ridout.

In 1843, John Howard designed a white-brick villa for Proudfoot, with a round-ended sitting room and boudoir at opposite ends of the ground floor and spacious chambers on the second. Thomas Storm was the builder. Three years later, Caroline and William moved into Kearnsey House — one of the grandest residences in Toronto at that time. The drawing room alone was an astonishing seventy-five by twenty-five feet.

Kearnsey House occupied a large property on the east side of Yonge Street that was originally granted to Captain George Playter. At the time it was built, the house was surrounded by open countryside, most of it later planted in orchards. The property extended to Church, and north from Wellesley almost to Bloor. The curving carriage drive entered from Yonge and swept in a large ellipse past the house. Elaborate ironwork pillars graced the verandah, while Ionic columns supported a second-floor balcony overlooking the lawns. Statues and urns were decoratively placed about the sculpted gardens.

The Proudfoots played host to many balls, musical evenings, and theatrical entertainments. Sumptuous dinners with Toronto's elite were de rigueur, but the glory days were coming to a close.

The Bank of Upper Canada was in dire financial straits during the late 1850s, even as a development boom boosted Toronto's economy. In 1861, a befuddled Proudfoot and his cashier, Ridout, stepped down. At the same time, Kearnsey House was bound over to the bank. The following year, Robert Cassels purchased the property.

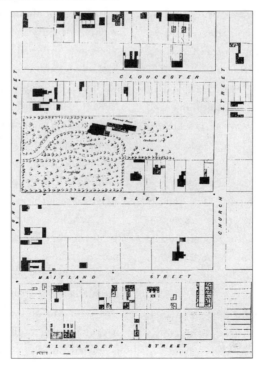

From the Boultons' Atlas of the City of Toronto (1858). Proudfoot's property was north of Wellesley and midway between modern Yonge and Church Streets. Today, Dundonald Street runs through the site of the house.

William Proudfoot built Kearnsey House between 1843 and 1846. The house was designed by architect John Howard of Colborne Lodge.
The drawing room alone was seventy-five by twenty-five feet. MTRL T11441

The last record of William Proudfoot was an 1866 deed of purchase for land north of Toronto. By the late 1860s, Proudfoot's wife was living in London as a woman of substantial means, and by 1872, Mrs. Proudfoot was referred to in directories as a widow. As the *Dictionary of Biography* puts it, Proudfoot "died, as he had lived, in conspicuous obscurity."

In 1869, Kearnsey House was sold again, this time to Donald Mackay. Mackay changed the name to Dundonald, and once more the house resounded to the sounds of spirited entertainments. Mackay

hosted a gathering of four hundred members of the General Assembly of the Church of Scotland in Canada at his spacious home. John Ross Robertson wrote in the late 1890s, "Kearnsey House, when first erected, was the finest residential building in the city, and even now, after fifty years, it still retains its character, as among the best of our citizens' homes."

The house was demolished in 1904. Dundonald Street runs through the site today.

HAZELBURN
Samuel Peters Jarvis

William Jarvis was a United Empire Loyalist who served as an ensign under Colonel Simcoe during the Revolutionary War. When the family's property in Connecticut was confiscated, William left for England, where he married Hannah Owen. After Simcoe was appointed Lieutenant-Governor, he designated Jarvis as Provincial Secretary and Registrar of Records. Secretary Jarvis was plagued by troubles in office. His task was to draw up land deeds and collect fees, but he seems to have been a habitual procrastinator, and his duties — and income — were curtailed under Peter Russell's administration.

Through a number of transactions, Jarvis received park lot 6, but considering it too far from the city to live, he built a comfortable house at Sherbourne and Adelaide. By 1803, Jarvis had cleared only twenty acres of his park lot. A first son, named Samuel, was born to the Jarvises, but he died young. The second son, born in 1792, was also named Samuel (both grandfathers were Samuels). Samuel Peters studied at Dr. Strachan's school in Cornwall. He served in the militia during the War of 1812 before becoming a lawyer and clerk of the Crown.

During William's last years, several civil suits for large sums were brought against him, so he turned over his real estate to Samuel. While Sam was in prison in 1818, awaiting trial over the Ridout duel, William Jarvis died. After his release that same year, Samuel married Mary Boyles Powell, a daughter of Chief Justice William Dummer Powell.

Samuel took over the post vacated by his father and assumed his park lot as well. He cleared the southern half of its original pine growth around 1822 and built his home, Hazelburn, in 1824. In January 1825, his mother-in-law wrote to her brother detailing how Mr. Powell's income had been reduced: "an unfortunate circumstance, as it reduces our ability to assist our daughter Mary in the furnishing for her new House, where they have now removed…."

The house was set well back from Lot Street on a slight rise visible from Lake Ontario's shoreline. Built by John Ewart, who later constructed Osgoode Hall and Upper Canada College, Hazelburn was an attractive two-storey brick dwelling with a large verandah that looked out over ten acres of well-kept lawns and gardens. The interior was panelled with black walnut. The drive entered at Lot Street (at the head of what later became Jarvis Street), ran over a bridge across the creek, past hazelnut trees, and circled in front of the door. The trees, along with a little burn that ran through the property, gave the estate its charming name.

The outbuildings at Hazelburn — the stables northwest of the house, a large hen house, a rabbit warren, and a smoke house — were also constructed of brick. Beyond the stables was wild bush where the family enjoyed excellent trout fishing. The Jarvises were renowned for their hospitality, and often held readings, musicales, and theatrical performances in which friends and neighbours took part.

In 1837, Samuel was appointed Chief Superintendent of

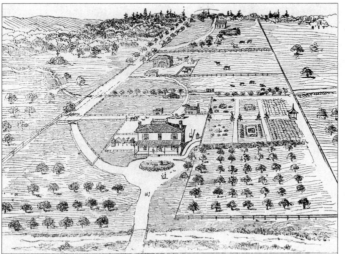

Samuel Jarvis's Hazelburn (from John Ross Robertson's Landmarks of Toronto, *Volume Two).*
The estate's name is taken from the hazelnut trees and the tiny stream or "burn" that ran behind the house.

LEFT: *When Jarvis Street was laid out up the middle of the property, most of Hazelburn was demolished. By the 1890s, when this photograph was taken, the upper end of Jarvis was one of Toronto's most prestigious residential areas.* MTRL 968-12-565 RIGHT: *Samuel Peters Jarvis (1792-1857) in his early sixties. Jarvis's mismanagement as Superintendent of Indian Affairs led to financial difficulties that forced him to subdivide his estate.* MTRL T30358

the Department of Indian Affairs. Five years later, a commission of inquiry investigated his department's activities. Jarvis was dismissed in June 1845, after an audit showed he personally owed the government £4,000. With seven children to support, Sam started to sever and sell lots.

Jarvis hired John Howard to survey Hazelburn for subdivision, which he did between 1846 and 1851. Howard laid out Mutual and George Streets, as well as Jarvis Street, a grand, eighty-foot-wide avenue with sixteen-foot boulevards. The house stood in the middle of the proposed road, so in 1847 most of it was torn down. A few rooms on the west side were later converted into a residence. Colonel Carthew salvaged the walnut panelling for his house on upper Yonge Street. William Cawthra invested £4,000 to develop the southern forty acres. In 1857, Samuel Peters Jarvis passed away.

The south end of Jarvis Street had small lots for working-class housing. The lots grew in size as they approached Bloor, where substantial one-acre parcels sold for $500 each. Here Toronto's industrial and mercantile elite — the Cawthras, the Masseys, the Mulocks, the Flavelles, and the McMasters — built their mansions. The 1878 *Illustrated Historical Atlas of the County of York* declared:

Jarvis Street is the handsomest avenue in Toronto and cannot perhaps be equalled on the continent. The well formed road, the boulevarded borders, and the delightful villas with their well ordered grounds, present to the eye a very attractive picture.

By the 1920s, fashionable society had moved on again, this time to Rosedale, Forest Hill, and Bayview. The face of Jarvis changed significantly as a result of demolitions following the Second World War.

MOSS PARK
William Allan

William Allan, born in Aberdeenshire, Scotland, in 1770, was the son of Alexander Allan of the Moss Farm. William settled first at Niagara, but arrived in York in 1795, where he was made the first postmaster and collector of customs. He made a significant portion of his wealth in the early years, outfitting the army and supplying the officers at Fort York, and he eventually became York's most prominent capitalist as a merchant and wholesaler.

Allan was a lieutenant colonel of the militia during the War of 1812. During the invasion of York, his possessions were looted. The compensation he received afterward allowed him to expand operations further. He was probably the wealthiest man in Upper Canada in his day, and his financial advice and management were eagerly sought by other members of the Family Compact.

Allan married Leah Gamble, a sister of Mrs. James Buchanan

Moss Park in 1842. This painting of William Allan's estate is attributed to James Hamilton. MTRL JRR T30698

Macaulay of Wickham Lodge. After first building a town house on Frederick Street, Allan acquired park lot 5 in 1819. In 1827, he started work on a spacious brick mansion on the west side of today's Sherbourne Street. The lot was covered in original pine forest. To the east was the Ridout estate, and on the west, Samuel Jarvis's Hazelburn. In March 1828, Mary Jarvis wrote to her mother, Mrs. Powell:

> Mr. Allan's new house is quite a palace and puts us completely in the back ground being three times the size of this and we think Mr. Allan promises himself some amusement in viewing the improvements made on Mr. Jarvis' premises as he has put twelve windows in the end of the house next to us — which gives it a very odd appearance.

Allan reportedly spent a princely £3,248 for the construction of Moss Park, and the same amount again for alterations and furnishings.

The house was built in the Greek revival style, with enormous columned pediments at either end. The residence faced east, and orchards and gardens lay to the north. The ample dining room was eighteen by twenty-four feet and the library was eighteen feet square. The Allans' palatial residence became the talk of York.

The Allans had ten children, but the winter of 1831–32 brought tragedy. Eight of the ten children died that winter of consumption, whooping cough, scarlet fever, and croup. Mrs. Powell wrote:

> Here is a lamentable proof of the insufficiency of wealth to promote or rather confer happiness; Allan from a state of indigence is one of the richest men in the community; his house as you know is a Palace; its splendour has become desolation.

This photograph was likely taken in 1893, after George William Allan, the only surviving child of ten, inherited Moss Park. MTRL T11102

Only one son, George William Allan, born in 1822, survived past childhood.

In addition to his business involvements, William Allan was a member of both the Legislative and Executive Councils, and a president of the Bank of Upper Canada. He continued to improve Moss Park through the 1830s and 1840s. John Howard designed the additions, including a portico for the front entry and a bath with running hot and cold water installed in 1841. In 1845, Howard surveyed and built a new road along the eastern boundary and laid out building lots. Known for years as Allan's Lane, it is now Sherbourne Street.

George Allan married in 1846. His father presented him with the north half of the Moss Park estate as a wedding gift.

William lived at Moss Park until his death in 1853. George then moved into the house and began dividing the bulk of the family property during the development boom of that period. In 1854, sixty-nine lots were laid out from present-day Dundas up to Gerrard for suburban villas. Two curved streets — Wilton and Wellesley Crescents — which were rare for the time, were opened. Pembroke was developed as a tree-lined avenue and was considered one of the city's finest residential streets in its day.

Most of Moss Park had gone to building lots by 1894, including the gardens. George died in 1901. His wife stayed another two years, but after a brief intervening ownership, the city acquired the house and demolished it. Although Moss Park Armoury preserves the estate's name, it actually stands on former Jarvis property.

THE HOME WOOD
George William Allan / Frederic Nicholls

In 1846, George William Allan married Louisa Robinson, daughter of Attorney General John Beverley Robinson. At that time, Allan's father presented him with fifty acres — the northern half of the Moss Park estate in park lot 5.

The Home Wood was built on the thickly wooded property between 1846 and 1847. The gate lodge that guarded the winding lane to the house stood on the north side of what is now Carlton Street. Brick stables and a coach house were in the rear. The house was a red-brick Gothic delight designed by architect Henry Bowyer Lane. Stone trim, delicate tracery, ornate vergeboards, and stained glass added to its period splendour.

Sadly, Louisa died of tuberculosis while on a honeymoon tour of Europe in 1852. Her generous father-in-law died the next year. Allan inherited the family homestead of Moss Park and moved back there.

George Allan remarried in 1857. He had four sons and three daughters with his second wife, Adelaide Schreiber, at Moss Park.

Adelaide's father, Rev. Thomas Schreiber, rented the Home Wood.

George Allan was a busy lawyer, politician, and prominent civic leader. He held a long list of executive positions over the years in many of Toronto's political and cultural organizations, including Mayor, City Councillor, Speaker of the Senate, Chancellor of Trinity College, and President of the Ontario Society of Artists. Fittingly, he donated five acres to the Horticultural Society for public gardens, and the Prince of Wales officially opened the gardens in 1860. A rustic pavilion of peeled logs was the centrepiece of the gardens. It was replaced by a larger structure in 1878, which served as a conservatory and concert hall. At the opening, it was announced that the beauty spot would thereafter be called Allan Gardens and it was a fashionable destination for promenades for many years. The second Pavilion burned down in 1902; the present palm house was erected seven years later.

Beginning in the late 1850s, Allan subdivided the forested land at the north end of Home Wood and opened up Huntley, Selby, Linden, and Isabella Streets. The house and remaining acreage were sold in 1863 to Benjamin Homer Dixon, Canadian Consul General of the Netherlands and brother of Harriette Boulton of the Grange. It was Dixon who changed the spelling to Homewood. The house was vacant from 1897 to 1900. Dixon then sold the property to Frederic Nicholls, electricity magnate and founder of what later became the Canadian General Electric Company.

The Nichollses kept up the stables and the greenhouse, and added a palm room replete with mosaic tile floor, wicker, and urns. They also added a billiard room on the northwest side of the house. The addition was decorated with moose,

Homewood's reception room during the Nicholls era.
Wellesley Hospital Archives, Wellesley Central Hospital.

The Homewood gates in 1912, when Dr. Herbert Bruce was preparing to open his private hospital in the grand residence. Wellesley Hospital Archives, Wellesley Central Hospital.

George William Allan (1822–1901), circa 1860. Allan built the Home Wood on the northern half of his father's estate, but he later inherited Moss Park. He was Mayor of Toronto in 1855 and Speaker of the Senate from 1888 to 1891. MTRL T34414

mountain goat, and elk trophies, as well as a priceless art collection that included Gainsboroughs and Turners. The family members were enthusiastic equestrians and kept a stable of fine mounts. A grass tennis court graced the east lawn.

During the Nichollses' occupancy, the Homewood was once again a hub of Toronto social life. In 1909, following Mrs. Nicholls's death, Dr. Herbert Bruce bought Homewood, where he opened the private, seventy-two-bed Wellesley Hospital in 1912.

Homewood was demolished in 1964 to make way for Wellesley Hospital expansion. Some windows from the Palm Room were incorporated into a hospital lounge. The front gates, adorned with the estate's name, were removed to a wrecking yard, where they were installed at the entrance and painted bright orange. Only Homewood Avenue remains to remind us of the romantic wooded estate of George Allan.

SHERBORNE VILLA
Thomas Gibbs Ridout / George A. Cox

Samuel Ridout bought park lot 4 from the estate of John White in 1818. Attorney General White was killed in York's first duel by Major John Small, Clerk of the Executive Council. The duel resulted after Mrs. Small and Mrs. Elmsley snubbed Mrs. White. Mr. White then began to circulate libellous stories about Mrs. Small, which her husband felt obliged to challenge. The duel took place on January 3, 1800.

Thomas Gibbs was the third son of Thomas Ridout, who had come to York in 1794. The father had filled a number of positions, including Commissariat, Surveyor General, and Registrar. Thomas Gibbs Ridout was born in 1792 and was named for his paternal grandmother, Mary Gibbs. He was educated at Dr. Strachan's school like the sons of other prominent Toronto families, and then appointed Deputy Assistant Commissary General for Upper Canada during the War of 1812. He remained in the commissariat until 1820, when he was retired on half pay. He married Anne Sullivan, but she died in 1832 leaving two sons and a daughter. Thomas had another five daughters and six sons with his second wife, Matilda-Ann Bromley.

In 1822, Ridout became Cashier for the newly formed Bank of Upper Canada. He held the position until 1861 and developed a reputation as a conscientious and respected businessman.

Thomas bought the western half of his half-brother Samuel's park lot. In 1845, he opened a road along the west lot line in conjunction with William Allan.

Allan gave a twenty-foot lane on the east side of his farm, while Ridout contributed a thirty-foot strip. Ridout then asked the city that it be called Sherborne Street. The later spelling incorporates a "*u*," which crept in inadvertently. Ridout proceeded to sell off most of his Sherborne Street frontage, reserving a large section for himself between Carlton and Howard.

In 1857, Thomas began building a grand home, which he called Sherborne Villa, after his father's birthplace in Dorset. The Italianate villa was designed by celebrated architect Frederick Cumberland, who was married to Mrs. Ridout's sister. It was an enormous white-brick house, more reminiscent of the Venetian countryside than its muddy York roots.

The Bank of Upper Canada faced a financial crisis in the late 1850s. Like the bank president, William Proudfoot, Ridout was forced to sell his estate even before the house was complete.

Thomas died on July 29, 1861. An announcement in the *Toronto Leader* two days later lamented, "Of unbending integrity and sterling honesty, Mr. Ridout was respected by all, being possessed of an amiable and generous disposition, he had many warm and attached friends." He left behind a widow and twelve children.

In 1867, Henry S. Howland, an industrialist with railroad interests, bought Sherborne Villa. He lived there for twenty years. During this period, development slowly spread out to the district. In 1888, Senator George Cox, a wealthy financier and noted Toronto philanthropist,

Thomas Gibbs Ridout (1792–1861) was forced to sell his Sherborne Villa when the Bank of Upper Canada, of which he was cashier, faced financial crisis in the late 1850s. MTRL JRR T14838

Sherborne Villa, circa 1910. Senator George Cox, head of a large financial empire that included the Bank of Commerce, National Trust, Dominion Securities, and Canada Life, was responsible for Sherborne Villa's opulence. CTA James 3120

purchased the house. By that time, Sherbourne had become a very fashionable address for Toronto's well-to-do.

During the Cox era, the house was used frequently for lavish receptions and dinners. Guests were received in the drawing room or music room, both of which had fifteen-foot ceilings and walls papered in green, watered silk. The dining room had rich, oak wainscotting and wine-hued, tooled Italian leather above. A stained-glass skylight illuminated the impressive staircase.

Senator Cox lived at Sherborne Villa until he passed away in 1914. Two years later, the house was purchased by Harris Henry Fudger, president of the Robert Simpson Company, to be used as a residence for out-of-town female employees.

When its residence days were over, the house was purchased by the city. It was demolished in 1964. Only Bleeker (named for Charlotte Bleeker Powell, who married a Ridout) and Sherbourne Streets remain.

DAVENPORT
Ensign John McGill / Joseph Wells

The escarpment north of York is the former shoreline of Lake Ontario's glacial predecessor, Lake Iroquois. With its wide panoramas, the ridge became popular with Toronto's propertied class, and a number of estates and mansions were built there. The first was Davenport. Later came others, such as Spadina, Russell Hill, Mashquoteh, Rathnelly, Oaklands, Glen Edyth, and — the best known of all — Casa Loma.

The first owner of lot 25, in the second concession from the Bay, was John McGill, an ensign with the Queen's Rangers, stationed at York. Some speculate that he named his two-hundred-acre farm lot after Major Davenport, who was an officer at the garrison at that time. Since patentees had to erect a house within a year to secure their deeds, McGill probably built his home in 1797. Modern Davenport Road, called the Plank Road for many years, was at that time a curving portage trail from the Don to the Humber and had been used by generations of Native people. The McGills would have enjoyed unobstructed views of the harbour and lake from their hilltop estate.

Joseph Wells was born in London in 1773, the son of a prosperous silk merchant. After purchasing a commission in 1798, Wells distinguished himself — and enjoyed rapid promotion — during the Napoleonic Wars, under the Duke of Wellington's command. He was the only officer in his battalion to survive Badajoz, where young Francis Simcoe and thousands of other British soldiers perished.

In 1813, Wells married Harriett King in London and shortly afterward was offered a post in Upper Canada as an inspector of the militia. Unfortunately, with the close of the war, the position was abolished on his arrival and he was retired on half pay. York residents thought highly of this hero in their midst. As John Ross Robertson put it, he was "a remarkably handsome man, the very essence of courtesy and of unsullied honour,"

As a retired British officer, Wells was entitled to substantial land grants. He also purchased Davenport in 1821, for £750, from Mrs. McGill, who was a widow by that time. The colonel built a much larger home on the original site, just west of modern Wells Hill Avenue, to the north of what would become Austin Terrace. He planted orchards and fields on the estate, and built stables northwest of the house.

The Wells, with eight sons and two daughters, were welcomed into York's social circle. The eldest son, George Dupont, was one of the first students at Upper Canada College. Colonel Wells sat on both the Legislative and Executive Councils of Upper Canada, was on the first board of directors of the Bank of Upper Canada when it was founded in 1821, and was appointed Bursar of King's College in 1828. A position as Treasurer at Upper Canada College ended in scandal in

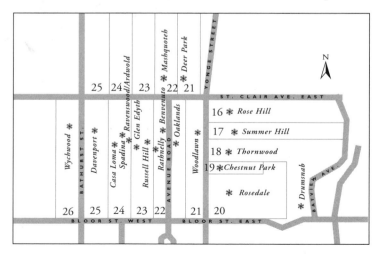

Many of the midtown estates were built on the Davenport escarpment. The First, Davenport, was followed by Spadina, Russell Hill, Rathnelly, Oaklands, Casa Loma, and others.

LEFT: *Davenport in 1894. By this time, the estate had dwindled to just a few acres and the surrounding district was already known as Wells' Hill.* MTRL T11544
RIGHT: *Colonel Joseph Wells, the second owner of lot 25, bought the two-hundred-acre lot in 1821 and built a larger house also named Davenport.*
This portrait was painted in 1835, when he was sixty-two years old. CTA SC 575 #1

1839. The school's funds were in complete disarray, which was not a wonder if rumours that he carried receipts and accounts around in his coat pocket were true. Wells was much better prepared for life as a gentleman farmer than as an accountant.

Colonel Wells died in 1853. His wife predeceased him by two years. The eldest son, George, passed away in 1854. The Davenport property was subsequently divided into three strips that ran from Bloor up to St. Clair. The eastern portion, with the house, went to the fourth son, Frederick. Robert, the second son, inherited the middle strip, and his descendants lived there until 1894. The western section went to the last surviving son, Arthur. By 1862, the area south of Wells Street had been subdivided into small building lots. The land between Wells Street and Dupont followed. The three north–south streets opened at that time were originally named George, Robert, and Frederick, but they were later changed to Albany, Howland, and Brunswick.

Frederick Wells, who also had an impressive military career, married Georgina Dartnell and had a son, George, in 1873, and a daughter, Nina, in 1875. Georgina died in childbirth and Frederick left Davenport, with his two young children, for England, where he died two years later. Robert's widow lived in the house with her second husband and family after Frederick's departure. By 1890, the estate had dwindled to just a few acres, but it had been joined on the escarpment by a number of other impressive properties — Spadina, Glen Edyth, Wychwood — and many more modest homes.

Nina Wells returned to Davenport in 1894 and married Adam de Pencier the following year. They lived at Davenport for ten years, but then moved to Manitoba and later British Columbia, where de Pencier became Archbishop. After renting out the property for three years, Nina sold Davenport in 1913. The house was demolished and the remaining property subdivided.

Albert Austin's Spadina, circa 1905, several years before the third floor was added. On the terrace, from left to right, are Albert Austin and James (standing), and Mary, Albert William, and a family friend (seated). In the foreground are Anna Kathleen (left), Constance Margaret (right), and Adele Mary (standing far right).

Toronto Historical Board, Spadina Collection.

SPADINA
William Warren Baldwin / James Austin

Widower Robert Baldwin, father of sixteen children, followed the Willcocks family from Ireland to Upper Canada in 1798. The eldest son was William Warren, a medical graduate of about twenty-four years of age. William started teaching in the house he rented in York and he studied law. Five years later, he married one of his landlord's daughters, Phoebe Willcocks.

William and Phoebe Baldwin inherited lot 24 in the second concession after her father died in 1813. Baldwin brought in a tenant farmer for a time, and then, in 1818, built a family home on the two-hundred-acre property. He called it Spadina (pronounced spadeena), after the Native term *espadinong*, meaning "hill." In addition to being a lawyer and a doctor, William was an amateur architect, and he designed the house himself. It was a two-storey, wood-frame building, somewhat plain, but very functional. He wrote in 1819:

> I have a very commodious house in the Country — I have called the place Spadina, the Indian word for Hill — or Mont — the house consists of two large Parlours Hall & stair case on the first floor — four bed rooms and a small library on the 2d. floor — and three Excellent bed rooms in attic storey or garret — with several closets on every storey — a Kitchen, dairy, root-cellar wine cellar & mans bed room underground — I have cut an avenue through the woods all the way so that we can see the vessells passing up and down the bay — the house is completely finished with stable &c and a tolerable good garden, the whole has cost about 1500£ the Land you know was the gift of poor Mr Willcocks.

William and Phoebe had five sons: Robert, Augustus, Henry, William, and Quetton St. George (who was named after Laurent Quetton St. George, a close family friend). Although the house was three miles from town, Baldwin declared, "[the trip,] often on foot, conduces much to the health of myself & my boys."

Northwest of the house was the barnyard, and a path led from the poultry shed to a creek at the base of the escarpment. Maria Willcocks, Phoebe's unmarried sister, lived at Spadina and used to walk the ducks and geese down to the water each day along this route. William later turned the goose walk into a picturesque trail with a rustic log shelter where the family kept a book of their own poems and witticisms. Baldwin also established a family burial plot called St. Martin's Rood.

Elizabeth Russell died in 1822, leaving most of her property to Phoebe Baldwin and Maria Willcocks. Dr. Baldwin again applied his designing talents as he started carving up the Russell property south of Bloor into residential lots. He planned a grand avenue as its centrepiece. In 1836, 132-foot-wide Spadina Avenue was laid out along the line between lots 14 and 15. Lined with imported chestnut trees, this fine thoroughfare presented a grand vista from Spadina House. The streets Baldwin opened were named for various family members: Baldwin, Russell, Robert, Phoebe, Heyden (now Sussex), Sullivan, St. George, Willcocks, and Maria (now Soho).

Over the years, Dr. Baldwin occupied a number of important public positions. He was a judge, Treasurer of the Upper Canada Law Society, and a member of the Legislative Council, in addition to

William Warren Baldwin (1775–1844), the first civilian doctor in York, was also a lawyer and a self-taught architect. Baldwin married Phoebe Willcocks, a cousin of Peter and Elizabeth Russell. Through Russell and Willcocks's connections, the Baldwins came to own several choice lots around present-day Toronto. MTRL JRR T31037

The front hall at Spadina in 1915. This view, published in Saturday Night, *shows the portrait of James Austin hanging partway up the stairs.*
Toronto Historical Board, Spadina Collection

carrying on both law and medical practices. He was a busy man, and in time the trip to the country home became less convenient. Spadina burned down in 1835, and William built a fine town home to avoid the uncomfortable and time-consuming commute. He lived at this new house at 44 Front Street West until his death. In 1836, he had a smaller country home built on the old Spadina foundations.

After Baldwin's death in 1844, his estate, including the town house, went to Robert as his eldest son. The fourth son, William Augustus, stayed on at Spadina with his large family until he built his own estate, Mashquoteh.

Robert was a prominent lawyer, and his unfailing efforts as a moderate Reformer earned him the epithet of "father of responsible government." He married his cousin, Augusta Elizabeth Sullivan, and they had four children: Phoebe, William Willcocks, Augusta, and Robert. He retired from politics in 1851 and spent much of his time at Spadina after that. According to his wishes, when he died in 1858, he was buried at St. Martin's Rood next to his late wife. Her letters were placed over his heart and his coffin was chained to hers.

After Robert's death, his surviving son, William Willcocks, began selling off the estate. Walmer Road was developed and named for the English birthplace of one of William's sons. The house and eighty remaining acres were sold at auction to James Austin in 1865 for £3,550, bringing the Baldwin years at Spadina to a close. Although the Baldwins had held a great deal of property, most of it was sold at times when prices were depressed. The family never capitalized on their real estate.

James Austin, born in Ireland, started in business as a grocer and later moved into finance. As a founder and president of Dominion Bank, he opened two branches in Toronto, ushering in the era of branch banking. Austin was also President of Consumers Gas. Austin demolished the second Spadina and built the present one in 1866. The new house incorporated the fieldstone foundations of the 1818 Baldwin house, while the dining room flooring is very likely from the second Spadina. The most visible relics of the original house are the former front door, sidelights, and fanlight, which now form the back entrance of the Austin house.

The Austins' Spadina — a grand Victorian home surrounded by gardens, groomed lawns, and majestic oaks — still stands today. The drawing room is forty-two feet long and features the original Jacques and Hay furniture, crystal gas lighting fixtures, and gilt-framed mirrors. Elaborate design details abound, such as the ornate, cast-iron radiator grilles and the keystones above the windows that depict native flora — trillium, lily of the valley, rose, thistle, and oak.

In 1889, James Austin subdivided the forty acres west of Spadina. Three years later he deeded twenty acres and the house to his son Albert. James died in 1897. His widow, Susan, moved into the cottage on the property to make way for her son and daughter-in-law and their growing family. Albert embarked on the first of three renovations. In 1898, a large addition, with a billiard room and a ground-floor kitchen, was made to the north. In 1905, the Austins added a palm room, a glassed porte-cochere, and terraces. By this time there were five children: James, Adele, Albert, Anna Kathleen, and Constance.

The Austins were frequent hosts, and Mrs. Austin was especially involved in Toronto's music life. In her autobiography, *Memory's Wall*, Flora Eaton wrote:

> Mr. and Mrs. Albert Austin, neighbours on our west, were friendly, open-handed hosts, of the type who would never let any disparity in age stand in the way of friendship…. One of their afternoon receptions, when Maggie Teyt, the British singer, was a special guest, lingers as a glowing picture in my mind: Mrs. Austin in beetroot velvet with rose-point collar and cuffs, earrings, bracelets and plastron of beautiful deep amethysts set in gold with diamonds; all the ladies in long dresses of satin or broadcloth, set off with fur stoles and occasionally a muff; a uniformity of white gloves and feather-trimmed hats. How one managed all this plus a cup of tea and other things, I can't quite remember, yet I know we all did — keeping our gloves on throughout. Gentlemen were present that day, as they almost always were at the Austins' teas, and they were equally correct in frock coats and Ascot ties. A fruit punch was often served, and sometimes it was flavoured with brandy, but liquor or cocktails were never offered to afternoon guests in Toronto homes at that time. The only exception was made during the Christmas season when trays of Madeira or Sherry would be passed to accompany the traditional Christmas cake.

The Austins were one of the first Toronto families with a telephone, and Albert had a separate cubicle built to house it. The family also had a makeshift golf course north of the house, which Albert formalized with the title Spadina Golf Club. The members of the club later relocated, forming the nucleus of the Lambton Golf Club. Albert added a third floor to Spadina in 1912, and fourteen years later he sold the north part of his property to the city for a reservoir.

Albert died in 1933. His second daughter, Anna Kathleen Thompson, lived in the house with her family from 1942 until 1982. Anna presented Spadina and its six-acre property to the city to be used as a historic house and museum. Spadina House opened in 1984, complete with much of the Austin furnishings, and it is maintained today by the Toronto Historical Board. Austin Terrace and Austin Crescent are also reminders of this leading Toronto family who occupied Spadina for four generations.

Augustus Baldwin's Russell Hill, circa 1870. The site is now Glen Edyth Place,
although Russell Hill Road perpetuates the name of the Admiral's estate. MTRL JRR T11117

RUSSELL HILL
Augustus Warren Baldwin

Admiral Augustus Warren Baldwin, born in 1776, was a younger brother of Dr. William Baldwin. A family history written in 1859 explains how Augustus joined the Navy. Apparently, while Robert Baldwin and his children were in England en route to Upper Canada, Augustus was approached by a press gang and made a midshipman. When the young man protested and explained who he was, the Admiral challenged "Well, Sir, and what objection have you to serve His Majesty?" "I have none, Sir, but my father does not wish it." "Your father is a fool, Sir," responded the Admiral. Young Baldwin was sent home for permission and, when he returned the following day, was given his commission. Augustus had an eventful career in the Navy and was promoted to Admiral before his retirement.

In 1817, Captain Baldwin, as he was then, joined the rest of his family at York. His brother already owned Spadina by that time and William spoke highly of the beautiful lot east of his own where he had often accompanied the Russells on walks. Augustus bought the two-hundred-acre "sugar loaf lot" from Elizabeth Russell and began to build a house in 1818. He named the property Russell Hill for his birthplace near Cork, Ireland, and in honour of the Russells. While his house and Spadina were under construction, Augustus and his brother lived at Davenport, which they rented from Mrs. McGill.

The house sat on the Davenport escarpment and looked down over York, three miles distant. It was a Regency style two-storey villa with a verandah. In 1827, Augustus married Augusta Melissa Jackson, daughter of John Mills Jackson. The Baldwins had one son and two daughters.

After he retired from the Navy in 1836, Augustus was appointed to Upper Canada's Executive Council. He held that position until the union of the Canadas in 1841. During those years, the two Baldwin households must have exchanged frequent visits. When Dr. Baldwin turned the goose path at Spadina into a sylvan promenade, Admiral Baldwin wrote this good-natured gibe for the family poetry volume:

The Gander's Lament

> I believe the good folks of Spadina are mad;
> If not mad their good sense strangely wanders
> To change into fairy land this piece of ground
> That was given to geese and to ganders.
> Must we tamely submit, must we give up our rights
> Without trying to break up this fiction?
> Can't we threaten a fight, turn rebels outright,
> Or consult Dr. B. 'bout an action?
> Then up stepped a grey headed gander and said: —
> "Good friends there is one way I'll show it,
> To keep our estate and secure us our bread
> 'Tis for every goose to turn poet."

Admiral Baldwin died at Russell Hill in 1866. All three of his children had predeceased him. After her husband's death, Augusta moved out of Russell Hill, and the house later burned to the ground. She sold several parcels of land before she died in 1870.

After Augusta's death, Augustus had willed his property to his brother's sons or, if deceased, to their heirs-at-law. Between 1870 and 1885, several parts of Russell Hill were sold off, including just over twenty-five acres to Samuel Nordheimer and twenty-two acres to Edmund Gunther. The proceeds were split into two shares, half going to William Augustus Baldwin and the other half divided among his late brother Robert's two daughters and son, William Willcocks Baldwin. William Willcocks appealed that, as his great-uncle's will had been written prior to the 1852 abolition of primogeniture, his siblings were not entitled to any of the property. The court ruled in his favour and his sisters were instructed to pay back the money.

Today, Admiral, Russell Hill, and Bedford Roads remain as reminders of Admiral Baldwin's Russell Hill estate.

DEER PARK
Agnes Heath / Charles Heath

The two-hundred-acre farm lot west of Yonge Street, in the third concession, was originally granted to Frederick Baron de Hoen. De Hoen was a German nobleman and officer with the mercenary Hessian troops who fought for Britain during the American Revolution. He sold most of the lot to Chief Justice John Elmsley's widow and she subsequently sold the southern forty acres to Agnes Heath for £1,050 in 1837. The property was roughly bounded by today's Yonge Street, Oriole Road, St. Clair Avenue, and Lonsdale Road.

The new owner was born Agnes Wallace in Arbroath, Scotland. She had married Colonel Heath, who served as an officer with the East India Company. Colonel Heath died in active service in Madras in 1818 and shortly afterward, Mrs. Heath took her three Indian-born children — Charles Wallace, Elizabeth Wallace, and Emily Mary — to Switzerland. From there she immigrated to Canada, settling first in Cobourg, where she built a fine house named Heathcote.

We can assume that Agnes Heath was a woman of significant social standing. While the family was in Cobourg, Emily Heath married D'Arcy Edward Boulton, the third son of D'Arcy Boulton Jr. of the Grange. Charles also married Sarah Ann Boulton, D'Arcy Edward's youngest sister. Charles became a barrister and moved to Toronto, and his mother and Elizabeth followed.

Agnes Heath named her new property Deer Park Farm. The house was near the corner of modern Deer Park Crescent and Heath Street West. Charles and his family appear to have lived there as well. The family kept a herd of tame deer on the property and in later years the animals would wander to the hotel at St. Clair and Yonge at dinnertime looking for handouts. At the top of a long rise from the lake, the house would have enjoyed a gorgeous view and lovely breezes. By the 1840s, the small community growing around the third concession road (St. Clair) and Yonge Street was known as Deer Park.

During Mackenzie's Rebellion of 1837, the Heaths could have looked out from their house to see Alderman John Powell, of Caer Howell, scouting up Yonge Street after receiving word of the rebel muster at Montgomery's tavern. Powell was captured, but with a concealed pistol he shot his guard at the Heaths' gate and galloped with word to town. Two days later, nine hundred men from the town, armed with two cannon, quelled the disorganized revolt just a mile north of Deer Park. Charles Heath, as befitting his conservative roots and connections, volunteered with the militia in 1837 and was promoted to Major.

In 1844, Agnes and her unmarried daughter, Elizabeth, moved back to Cobourg. Two years later, Charles bought the Deer Park estate from his mother and began to sell parcels. In 1847, Colonel Arthur Carthew bought six acres at the northeast corner of the Heath estate and named the magnificent house he built Lawton Park. John Howard designed the building and was

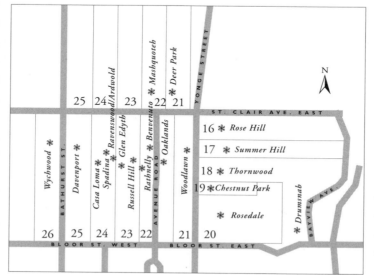

The area that has been known for more than 150 years as Deer Park took its name from Agnes Heath's estate.

John Fisken's Lawton Park, circa 1896. The house, which stood at the northwest corner of Heath Street West and Yonge, was built by Colonel Carthew on a six-acre parcel purchased from Charles Heath. Interior woodwork was salvaged from Sam Jarvis's Hazelburn. MTRL T11217

responsible for salvaging the walnut woodwork from Sam Jarvis's Hazelburn, which was demolished that year. Sadly, Carthew's fiancée was fatally injured on the property, and Carthew never lived there. In 1850, John Fisken, a prominent businessman, and founder of the Imperial Bank, purchased Lawton Park. That same year, Charles Heath registered a plan for subdivision. The lots south of Lawton Park were further subdivided after 1874. By 1908, the Deer Park area was annexed to the city.

No pictures of Deer Park exist today, and only Deer Park Crescent and Heath Streets remain as reminders of the original property.

Woodlawn's east facade before a kitchen wing was added on the left in the 1890s.
The altered home, still a private residence, is now accessed from Woodlawn Avenue. MTRL X 80

WOODLAWN
William Hume Blake / Joseph Morrison

Lots 21 and 22, in the second concession from Toronto Bay, were granted first to David Smith, Surveyor General. He sold these two lots on the west side of Yonge to Chief Justice John Elmsley. In 1838, Captain John Elmsley, who had inherited the land, sold a twelve-acre parcel to William Hume Blake. The property, which had Yonge Street frontage and was a quarter of a mile deep, was a heavily treed lot.

William Blake was born in Ireland in 1809, and was educated in law at Trinity College, Dublin. He came to Canada in 1832 and by 1838 had opened his own law office in Toronto. He later developed a very successful practice with his partner, Joseph Curran Morrison, and both were noted for their high spirits and clever wit. Blake was later made Chancellor of Upper Canada in 1849.

In September 1840, Blake had John Howard design a house for him on the Yonge Street property. A two-storey Regency villa finished in grey roughcast, the house's massive front entry was flanked by two sets of French doors. The inside featured rich walnut woodwork and a grand ballroom. Blake named the house Woodlawn.

In 1844, Blake sold Woodlawn to Joseph Morrison. The following year, Joseph married Elizabeth, daughter of Joseph Bloor of Yorkville. The Morrisons had three sons and three daughters at Woodlawn, and, wrote Donald Jones, "in the years between 1840 and 1880, their home on the hill with its great ballroom and conservatory was a centre of all that was fashionable in the life of this city."

Some time between 1853 and 1856, Morrison commissioned William Mundie, the outstanding landscape architect of his time, to design a forty-by-fifty-foot greenhouse.

In 1863, Morrison was appointed Chancellor of the University of Toronto and to the Queen's Bench. In 1877, he was made a judge of the Court of Appeal. Gracious entertainments were regular events at Woodlawn, including a traditional champagne breakfast for Upper Canada's judges and their friends every first of July.

Justice Morrison died at Woodlawn in 1885 and his executors divided the estate into six portions. A plan to subdivide twenty-one lots on Yonge Street and seventy-one lots on the north side of Walker was registered in 1886. Most of the lots went to the builder who constructed the homes. With subdivision, Woodlawn lost several outbuildings and its western wing. Angus Morrison inherited the diminished house and added a two-storey wing in 1895 to accommodate a new kitchen with bedrooms above.

Angus died in 1899. The house was rented for a number of years and greatly altered. In 1920, Bernard Saunders purchased the house and began restoring it.

Today, Woodlawn stands on five-eighths of an acre, but the house is only one-third its original size. Owned by Guy Saunders, Woodlawn is Toronto's second oldest residence still in use as a private home.

Yorkville.
From the *Illustrated Historical Atlas of the County of York* (1878).

William Augustus Baldwin was Dr. Baldwin's fourth son. Although his father's holdings went to the eldest son, Robert Baldwin,
William Augustus received three hundred acres of former Russell property in the third concession from his aunt and mother.

From the *Illustrated Historical Atlas of the County of York* (1878). MTRL T11119

MASHQUOTEH
William Augustus Baldwin

In *Toronto of Old*, Henry Scadding described Mashquoteh as "a colony transplanted from the neighbouring Spadina...." William Augustus Baldwin was the fourth son of Dr. William Warren Baldwin, who, through his wife's inheritance of the Russell estate, had considerable land holdings around York.

Robert Baldwin, as the eldest son, was to inherit his father's property. Fortunately for William, when he married Isabella Buchanan in 1834, his Aunt Maria Willcocks gave him lot 23 in the third concession, which she had inherited from the Russells. William and Isabella continued to live at Spadina as their family grew. Later, his mother added her half of lot 22 to William's adjoining property.

In 1850, Baldwin approached John Howard to draw up plans and erect, as the architect put it, "a large dwelling place at Deer Park for William Augustus Baldwin, Esq." The home was two and a half miles north of city. Isabella never saw the completed house; she died that year. William moved in with his five sons and two daughters.

The Native name for this lightly wooded plateau was *Mashquoteh*, which means "meadow where the deer come to feed." Baldwin used the name for his two-and-a-half-storey roughcast farmhouse. The front wall, facing west, stood in the middle of today's Avenue Road, just north of modern Heath Street. The gate lodge stood where Oriole Road and St. Clair Avenue intersect. The house was constructed of huge timbers cut from elms and oaks on the property. French windows opened onto encircling verandahs edged with scalloped fretwork. Many pieces of fine furniture came from Peter Russell's estate. The stables, cowsheds, henhouse and other outbuildings were north of the house. Beyond the gardens stood virgin forest. William worked at his farm, transforming it over time from bush land into valuable real estate.

In 1852, William remarried. With Margaret Macleod he had another nine children, all born at Mashquoteh. For more than thirty years, William kept the family residence and three-hundred-acre farm intact.

William died at Mashquoteh in 1883, and his estate was subdivided. The house was demolished in 1888 for the extension of Avenue Road. Thirty acres were sold to Upper Canada College, where the present campus opened in 1891. Heath Street was also extended westward at about this time to Forest Hill Road. A dip on Heath Street indicates where the creek behind Mashquoteh used to run.

In 1892, Margaret built another house called Mashquoteh on a large block bounded by Avenue Road, Heath Street, Forest Hill Road, and St. Clair Avenue. She lived there with her son Laurence and his family.

Eventually Mashquoteh was subsumed by the Village of Deer Park. Deer Park was annexed in 1908, and Margaret died the following year. The house was sold. It was finally demolished in 1956 to make way for apartments.

After Margaret Baldwin died, Laurence built two successive houses on Baldwin property, naming them both Mashquoteh. He continued to sell off pieces of his land, and many large homes were built in what became the Village of Forest Hill.

William Augustus Baldwin's residence at Deer Park was called Mashquoteh, from a Native phrase meaning "meadow where the deer come to feed." Shown here during the 1870s, the Mashquoteh site is now on Avenue Road, south of Heath Street. MTRL T11118

Rathnelly in 1897, when it was owned by Senator James Kerr. William McMaster named his country estate after Rathnally House, his Irish ancestral home not far from Dublin. The residential area surrounding the site today perpetuates the Rathnelly name. MTRL T33394

RATHNELLY
William McMaster

William McMaster, like his Baldwin neighbours, was also an Irishman. Born in Tyrone, Ireland, in 1811, he emigrated as a young man and settled at York in 1833. He began as a clerk in the wholesale and retail dry goods business owned by Robert Cathcart. In 1834, he was promoted to partner. Ten years later, he struck out on his own in the wholesale business. The venture was very successful, probably due to McMaster's diligence and persistence. In *Spadina: A Story of Old Toronto*, Austin Seton Thompson described McMaster as follows: "With a massive head sunk on a heavy neck he invited comparison with a bulldog, with which he shared in equal measure the qualities of stubbornness and tenacity."

By the late 1840s, McMaster's firm supplied goods to most of western Ontario's merchants. He was able to persuade two nephews to join him in William McMaster & Nephews, allowing him to retire from dry goods and pursue interests in the world of finance.

In 1851, William married Mary Henderson of New York City. Shortly after, he purchased property from St. James' Cathedral on the edge of the escarpment above Davenport Road. Lot 22 was originally Elmsley property, but the Chief Justice had presented it to St. James. McMaster named his estate Rathnelly (or Rathnally according to some sources) for his birthplace in Ireland.

The tablelands above Davenport were already known as the poplar plains by the time the McMasters arrived. They reached their country property along a winding dirt road that led from Davenport to the second concession road (now St. Clair Avenue). Rathnelly stood just east of this road, close to the west lot line. By 1877, maps showed the former by-road as Poplar Plains Road. The McMasters also built a mansion in 1860 on Bloor Street, at the highly fashionable north end of Jarvis. Mary died in 1868. Three years later, McMaster married Susan Moulton.

William was a founder and first president of the Bank of Commerce, which soon grew to become the city's largest banking house. He ran as a Liberal and won a seat in the legislature. After Confederation, he was made a senator.

McMaster was a fervent Baptist and a generous benefactor, contributing to the Baptist college, McMaster Hall (which opened on Bloor Street in 1881), and the Jarvis Street Baptist Church. He was also Treasurer for the Upper Canada Bible Society.

McMaster split up Rathnelly and called for tenders shortly before he died. The property south of the hill went to speculators. The senator died in 1887. Senator James Kerr purchased the Rathnelly house in about 1888 and lived there until his death in 1916. Simeon Janes purchased five and a half acres on Avenue Road, where he later built his Benvenuto.

Mrs. McMaster willed the Bloor Street home to McMaster University, and a Baptist girls' school, Moulton College, was opened there. When the school finally closed in 1954, a stained-glass window from the front hall was moved to McMaster University in Hamilton.

Poplar Plains Road and Poplar Plains Crescent roughly mark the site of the McMasters' summer home, and Rathnelly and McMaster Avenues immortalize one of Victorian Toronto's most successful capitalists.

OAKLANDS
John Macdonald

John Macdonald was born in Perthshire, Scotland, in 1824. His mother died when he was thirteen years old and he was raised by his stern father. John came to Upper Canada when his father's regiment was sent out to quell the 1837 Rebellion.

John was a serious young man when he took a position as a clerk in a dry goods firm in York. He converted to Methodism in 1842 and hoped to become a preacher, but tuberculosis forced him to give up that dream, as he was too weakened to withstand the requisite travel.

In 1849, John opened his own small dry goods shop on Yonge Street, south of Richmond, outside of the established commercial district. His biographer, Reverend Hugh Johnston, wrote:

> John Macdonald possessed in an eminent degree all the qualities which make a merchant prince. The corner-stone of his character was an earnest religious belief; and while his piety was of a rich and ardent type, he also had an integrity as firm as a rock, and an honour as unsullied as the stars.

In 1850, John married Eliza Hamilton. Three years later he opened a wholesale business. Even through the depression of the late 1850s, Macdonald's business prospered under his conservative management. By 1860, it had become the largest dry goods firm in Canada. Eliza died in 1850, leaving two children. John married Annie Alcorn in 1857 and had five daughters and five sons.

In 1858, Macdonald bought three blocks from the Anglican Church. The property, east of the extension of College Avenue as it was known until 1862, totalled thirty-five acres, reaching from Cottingham Street beyond today's Balmoral Avenue. He named it Oaklands for the trees on the estate.

The property was well outside the city in those days and not always easy to reach. A long drive approached from Yonge — now Cottingham — for in bad weather, Avenue Road was deeply rutted and impassable. The gates still stand on Oaklands Avenue. A son recalled in a letter to T. A. Reed in 1926, "I remember well my mother stating that she hardly felt like speaking to them [the land agents] as they were the ones who had induced my father to live so far in the country."

Oaklands was designed by architect William Hay in 1860. It was the first brick house built north of Bloor Street on Avenue Road and one of Toronto's finest residences. It was a Gothic-inspired two-storey home. Inside were an elaborately carved oak staircase, marble fireplaces, and high ceilings crowned with ornate mouldings. A landmark octagonal tower was added in 1870. Trim gardens surrounded the house, including an entire acre planted in strawberries and asparagus. The large stables and coach house were situated northeast of the house. From the dining and drawing rooms, where they frequently entertained, the Macdonalds had a spectacular view of the lake. From the tower, they could see Brock's Monument at Queenston Heights.

The Macdonalds, with a growing family, continued to make additions and renovations to Oaklands. Some pieces of land along the east and south were sold, and a new entrance was opened from newly developed Alcorn Avenue. Wrote James Timperlake in 1877:

John Macdonald (1824–1890). This photograph was likely taken in 1889, two years after Macdonald, both a Liberal and an opponent of Confederation, was appointed to the Senate by Sir John A. Macdonald. MTRL T13729

Oaklands, circa 1905, while Mrs. Macdonald and her children were still in residence. Above the main-floor windows at far left is a carved relief of a winged ship and a severed hand grasping a dagger. Family lore has it that a Macdonald once raced an adversary to claim a Scottish island; the man who first touched its shore would win. To ensure victory and secure the island for his descendants, the Macdonald cut off his hand and threw it ashore.
National Archives of Canada,
John Macdonald Collection. PA119996

The visitor in passing this delightful spot is at once struck with its beauty, which conveys the idea that one is in some pleasure grounds, as most assuredly it must be to the family residing therein."

In addition to running John Macdonald and Co., John was a director of the Bank of Commerce with his neighbour William McMaster. He was also an active supporter of many Toronto institutions, including the Methodist Church, Toronto General Hospital, the Bible Society, the Salvation Army, and Victoria College. He had more than thirty silver trowels given to him from cornerstone layings at which he officiated.

John Macdonald was elected to parliament in 1861. He opposed Confederation, but in spite of his opposition and his being a Liberal, he was appointed to the Senate in 1887. Above all, though, Macdonald was a devoted family man. He enjoyed playing marbles and chess with his children and leading regular family prayers and scripture readings.

Macdonald died in 1890. Annie lived at Oaklands with her children for another fifteen years. During that time, the city bought four acres for a park. In 1905, the estate of Cyrus McCormick, of American farm machinery fame, bought the remaining Oaklands property. A daughter, Mary Virginia McCormick, lived there for many years. Miss McCormick added several rooms, bay windows, and a bowling alley. Her alterations gave a jumbled appearance to the newer wing, but the porte-cochere was an attractive addition. In 1931, the Brothers of the Christian Schools bought the house and thirteen and a half acres from Miss McCormick for what is now De La Salle College Oaklands. Classes were held in the house and former stables until a modern school building was erected in 1949.

Today, John Macdonald's mansion is a residence for the Christian Brothers. It received Toronto Historical Board designation as a heritage property in 1996, and with its carefully restored slate roof and vergeboards, it is a Victorian treasure.

RAVENSWOOD
Anne Austin Arthurs

Margaret Georgina Arthurs and her wedding party at Ravenswood, 1894. Anne Austin Arthurs, the mother of the bride, is in the second row, at the far right.
James and Susan Austin, of Spadina, the bride's maternal grandparents, are seated. Anne Arthurs left Ravenswood in 1908.
It was eventually demolished to make way for the Eatons' Ardwold. Toronto Historical Board, Spadina Collection.

In June 1867, James Austin's daughter, Anne, and her husband, George Arthurs, decided to build a home on the Spadina property. The house was just 150 yards east of Spadina, close to the lot line of Russell Hill. The buff-brick mansion shared a drive with the family home. By 1889, Anne Arthurs was a widow, but she continued to offer her home and grounds for charitable events. There were bazaars and garden parties with Japanese lanterns, marquees, and military bands. The *Commemorative Biographical Record of the County of York, Ontario*, of 1907, described Ravenswood as "one of the most beautiful spots in the city of Toronto and Lake Ontario." Anne Arthurs sold Ravenswood in 1908 to John Craig Eaton.

E. R. Woods's Glendon Hall is now Glendon College, York University.
Today it houses the principal's residence, bookstore, gallery, offices, and cafe. The Woods' rose terrace has been restored at the southeastern end of the house.
Photograph by Donald Standfield.

Windfields is home to the Canadian Film Centre at 2489 Bayview Avenue.
E. P. Taylor's family stables immediately right of the house have been converted to a media centre.
Photograph by Liz Lundell.

Drumsnab is the oldest residence still in use as a private home in Toronto.
Francis Cayley's murals have been preserved inside.
Photograph by Donald Standfield.

The Ashbridge house on Queen Street East. A second storey and mansard roof were added in 1899, and a wing to the rear was built in the early 1900s.
The house is probably the oldest private home in Toronto that has been occupied continuously by the same family.
Photograph by Donald Standfield.

Oaklands, now a residence for the Christian Brothers, is part of the De La Salle College Oaklands campus.
From the octagonal tower, the Macdonalds enjoyed a panoramic view of the city and Lake Ontario.
Photograph by Donald Standfield.

J. S. McLean was president of Canada Packers when he commisioned Eric Arthur to design Bayview in 1928.
The home has been restored and is now used as a special events facility by Sunnybrook Health Science Centre.
Photograph by Donald Standfield.

Casa Loma's architect, E. J. Lennox was inspired by European castles. Work began in 1910, but Henry Pellatt was forced to abandon the extravagant residence in 1923 as taxes rose and his business failed. Building was never completed.

Photograph courtesy Casa Loma.

The Frank P. Wood house from the eastern, garden face. Wood's Bayview Heights home housed an impressive fine art collection that included works by Hals, Gainsborough, and Rodin. He left his residence and art collection to the Toronto Art Gallery (now the AGO).
Photograph by Liz Lundell.

GLEN EDYTH
Samuel Nordheimer

Samuel Nordheimer, the seventh of eight sons, was born into a Jewish family of wealthy Bavarian merchants in 1824. He and his brother Abraham immigrated to New York in 1839 to join an older brother who was a professor there. Abraham moved to Kingston to become a music tutor for a prominent family, and Samuel followed.

The brothers established a music business in Kingston in 1841, importing pianos and other instruments. The venture was highly successful. They transferred headquarters to Toronto in the early 1860s and opened branches in Hamilton, London, Kingston, Montreal, and Quebec. In later years, they manufactured pianos. The brothers also supported musical societies and clubs, built music halls, and arranged concerts — such as Jenny Lind's Toronto performance in 1853 — to further musical education in Canada. Abraham died in 1860 and was succeeded by his son, Albert. In addition to his music business, Samuel was a founder and director of several financial institutions.

Early in 1871, Samuel purchased just over twenty-five acres of the Russell Hill property from Admiral Baldwin's estate. In December of that year, he converted to the Church of England and married the beautiful Edith Louise Boulton, daughter of James Boulton and a niece of D'Arcy Boulton Jr. A pretty glen at the south end of the new property provided inspiration for the estate's name.

Edith and Samuel drew up a marriage contract. In it, Samuel pledged the land and house to Edith for his life and as long as she lived as his widow. He also specified that at least $25,000 would be spent on furnishings for their home.

The Nordheimers demolished the admiral's house and built a new one in 1872, close to the lot line and only a hundred feet east of Ravenswood. A Viennese architect designed the thirty-five-room mansion, with turrets, a widow's walk, a porte-cochere, and towers.

The Glen Edyth grounds were reminiscent of a grand English country estate. Stables, two coach houses, summerhouses, a cowshed, greenhouses, and kitchen gardens were situated on the property. A celebrated landscape architect was brought in from Cleveland to design the twenty-three acres of gardens. He dammed Castle Frank stream, which ran through property, to create a picturesque duck pond and waterfall. Urns, rustic bridges, and careful planting completed the park-like effect. James Timperlake described Glen Edyth in 1877 as follows:

> [Glen Edyth is] a beautiful residence built in the French style of architecture. The approach to the mansion is so constructed that as one crosses the many rustic bridges with their silvery stream bubbling beneath, it makes one fancy he is in fairy land…. It is, with the exception of Sir Hugh Allan's residence in Montreal, the most superb in all the Dominion.

As Consul for Germany, Samuel Nordheimer entertained thousands of guests, including the Duke of Connaught. Goldwin Smith of the Grange was a close friend. Lady Eaton, the Nordheimers' neighbour to the west, recalled:

Samuel Nordheimer (1824–1912). With his brother Abraham, Samuel established a prominent music business in Canada. From Men of Canada.

The Nordheimers' Glen Edyth. Built in 1872 on part of the earlier Russell Hill estate, Glen Edyth was one of the most impressive houses in Canada in its day.
From Lucy Booth Martyn's *100 Years of Grandeur: The Inside Stories of Toronto's Great Homes and the People Who Lived There.*

The gate lodge at Glen Edyth housed the gardener on one side and the coachman on the other.
Both apartments had four bedrooms and a fourteen-by-eleven-foot drawing room. MTRL T33470

Their house was large and distinguished, and I can remember great afternoon receptions there, and weddings and one or two balls…. Glen Edythe's grounds were a beautiful natural park. The gate lodges stood imposingly at the main entrance from Davenport Road, and in those early days only carriages, or sleighs in winter, used that driveway.

There were balls, dinner parties, and musical performances in addition to teas and receptions.

Both Mr. and Mrs. Nordheimer died in 1912. They had had eleven children, but only one son, Roy Boulton Nordheimer, survived them. Wrote Lady Eaton:

After the older Nordheimers' deaths, their son Roy brought his pretty bride to live there. Again there were gay parties, but by that time I was of the older generation and my contacts with Glen Edythe continued on a formal plane with an exchange of calls at intervals.

Roy lived at Glen Edyth until 1924.

Roy laid out some building lots in 1923, just before his death. His executors tried to sell Glen Edyth to the city as a park, but the property proved too expensive. The land was subsequently subdivided in the late 1920s. The house stood vacant until it was demolished in 1929 to make way for Glen Edyth Place. Boulton and Glen Edyth Drives mark the carriage entries to the old estate.

WYCHWOOD
Marmaduke Matthews

Marmaduke Matthews was born in 1837 in Warwickshire, England. He came to Toronto in 1860 after training as an artist, and in 1864, he eloped with Cyrilda Bernard. The couple fled from her father's wrath to the United States, but they returned to Toronto with several children in tow a number of years later. Matthews was a founding member of the Ontario Society of Artists in 1872, and was appointed President in 1894. As official artist for the Canadian Pacific Railway in the late 1880s and 1890s, he became well known for many of his landscapes of western Canada.

In 1873, Matthews bought ten acres, in the north part of lot 26 in the second concession, for $4,000. The next year, he built his home at the crest of the hill, naming it Wychwood for a woodland close to his childhood home. In those days, the approach to Wychwood was from Davenport. Wychwood originally had twelve rooms, but Matthews added another wing in 1877. The house had huge French doors, and in spite of full-length shutters, the odd cow would occasionally poke her nose in. Stables and gardens stood northwest of the house. Beyond was forest.

In 1877, Matthews and Alexander Jardine bought another twelve acres to the west of Wychwood, where Jardine built his home, Braemore Gardens. The two lots formed a block bounded by today's Bathurst Street, Davenport Road, Christie Street, and St. Clair Avenue.

Matthews and Jardine envisioned a co-operative artists' colony on the property. They filed a plan of subdivision in 1888. At the centre was a private park for residents, through which Taddle Creek flowed. Matthews and Jardine later dammed the stream to form a picturesque pond, the centrepiece of this pastoral enclave. In 1891, a revised plan incorporated more land divided into smaller lots and included building restrictions and provisions for a trusteeship.

For the first fifteen years, only Matthews and Jardine family members lived at Wychwood Park. The pond, much larger than it is today, was used for skating parties and swimming, and supplied the Matthews and Jardine homes with ice. Matthews also tinkered with mechanical inventions. While he was demonstrating a miner's lamp one day, a companion averted an explosion by grabbing the malfunctioning contraption and tossing it into the pond.

To augment his income from painting, Matthews worked as drawing master at St. Alban's Cathedral School, where his son was headmaster. Some St. Albans students boarded at Wychwood, and pupils frequently came to Wychwood's pond for swimming or sketching lessons.

The first wave of construction in Wychwood Park began in 1906, when artist George Reid built his home there. Reid's Tudor home — with its stucco and half-timbering, and charming, natural gardens — set the style for many of the homes that followed. Architect Eden Smith designed many of the houses in the Park in the English cottage style, and he built his own residence there in 1907. Artist Gustav Hahn, famous for his Art Nouveau designs, also made his home at Wychwood Park. High gables, leaded glass, oak-panelled inglenooks, ivy, and perennial borders created an old English feel.

Marmaduke Matthews (1837–1913) was official artist for the Canadian Pacific Railway in the late 1880s and 1890s. MTRL 975-7-1

Wychwood in 1984.
Photograph by Keith Miller, with permission from the Wychwood Park Archives. MTRL T30853

In 1907, Matthews, experiencing financial difficulties, mortgaged the twenty-two-acre property to the newly formed Wychwood Park Corporation. Two years later, the area was annexed to the city.

Marmaduke Matthews died in 1913. The lapsed 1891 trust deed was reinstated in 1917, and since that time an elected board of trustees has maintained roads, lighting, tennis courts, and other communal concerns. Matthews's daughter Alice lived in the family home until 1960. Subsequent owners have restored and carefully maintained it.

In 1985, Wychwood Park became the first residential area to receive heritage designation under the Ontario Heritage Act.

Today, visitors to Wychwood Park are struck by the serenity of this shaded enclave. The pond is somewhat smaller than in Matthews's day, but the descendants of goldfish deposited by a grandson on the eve of his departure for the First World War still swim there. Wild columbine grow along the banks of the pond, swans glide tranquilly across its surface, and idyllic bird song replaces the frenetic noise of the city, which seems miles away.

BENVENUTO
Simeon James

Simeon Janes's property was originally part of Senator McMaster's Rathnelly estate. Janes strolled up the Avenue Road hill one day, and pausing to admire the view, decided to build a house there. In 1888, he purchased five and a half acres of the McMaster estate from the new owner, James Kerr.

Janes was born in 1843 to a Loyalist family. His father was a farmer, but Simeon was educated at Victoria University, where he received a B.A. in 1866 and an M.A. in 1872. In 1867, he married Maria Ann Quinlan, and they later had one son, who died in infancy, and two daughters. Although his family had hoped Simeon would become a lawyer, he was more interested in business. He started first in dry goods, but in 1867 he found his true calling and embarked on a career in real estate development.

Janes made his fortune during the building boom of the late 1880s and early 1890s, developing the Annex. Recognizing its future potential, he had purchased former Baldwin property when prices were depressed. As the city spread, he then developed and aggressively promoted his subdivisions. Janes laid out most of the Annex from Avenue Road to Spadina south of Dupont. The lots were intended for comfortable middle-class homes, and Janes's plans eliminated laneways, which he felt were unnecessary and unsanitary. The *Cyclopaedia of Canadian Biography* of 1886 described Janes as "one of the most far-seeing, shrewd, and successful men of business in the community ... his operations are identified with the progress of the city

which he has chosen as the field of his enterprise." One of the first real estate developers to advocate skyscrapers for downtown Toronto, Janes was noted for his daring and far-sightedness, which he combined with sound judgement. Balancing his development genius was a genuine love of art and fine objects; Janes established many awards and scholarships in fine arts and received a Doctor of Laws in 1896 for his support of the arts.

The Janeses' home was built on the west side of Avenue Road, south of modern Edmund Street. John Macdonald's Oaklands was directly across Avenue Road. Benvenuto, which means "welcome" in Italian, was designed by architect Stanford White, designer of Madison Square Gardens. The house was built of solid-looking limestone, and deep windows and a red-tiled roof contributed to its massive, Norman appearance. The entrance was on the east side and was covered by a porte-cochere.

Inside, Janes commissioned Gustav Hahn to create Art Nouveau murals on the billiard room walls. The walls in the entry hall were panelled up to eight feet, with embossed leather above. Imported rare tapestries from Italy hung in the dining room, and the drawing room was resplendent in Louis XVI decor.

Along the west side of the house, the drawing room, music room, and main hall each looked out on conservatories. South of the house was a piazza with a low stone wall. The front gates at Benvenuto, of hand-crafted wrought iron, were made by a

Simeon Janes's Benvenuto, west of Avenue Road, south of modern Edmund Avenue. This photograph by Josiah Bruce shows the dining room some time between 1890 and 1897, after the house was purchased by Sir William Mackenzie. MTRL T11355

LEFT: *Taken about the same time as the interior shot.*
A sample of the massive stonework of Benvenuto is preserved in a garden wall along Avenue Road. MTRL T11350
RIGHT: *Simeon Janes developed and promoted most of the Annex and was considered a real estate genius.*
He was also a devoted patron of the fine arts. From Men of Canada.

Sienna artist. They depicted the goddesses of painting, sculpture, industry and mechanics. Wrote G. Mercer Adam in 1891:

> The site is commanding, and the mansion is a worthy, and likely to be a lasting adornment of its fine situation … approached by a winding drive from the massive lodge, with its beautiful gates and curved stone wall that flank the grounds on Avenue Road. It is a splendid piece of masonry, which puts to shame the flimsy ephemeral edifices, with their stuccoes and veneers, of modern house construction.

For the property and house, Janes paid a whopping $138,000.

In 1897, Janes sold the estate to railway-magnate William Mackenzie for $100,000 in railway stock. The stock rallied before Janes disposed of it, but he still took a loss of $13,000 on Benvenuto. Mackenzie, who was knighted in 1911, added a new wing to the already enormous home, and Benvenuto continued to occupy a position of social prominence in the city. Mackenzie also had the streetcar line — which he controlled — extended past Benvenuto up to St. Clair Avenue.

Mackenzie died at Benvenuto in 1923. In 1924, the estate was subdivided and the house demolished. The ornate gates were moved to 40 Burton Road, and the roof tiles were salvaged for a summer home on Lake Simcoe. The gate lodge was used as a tearoom for a number of years, but it too was demolished in 1932.

Eventually, fashionable apartments went up on much of the site. Edmund Street runs between where the house and stables stood. Benvenuto Place is also on the former estate, and the wall Simeon Janes built along Avenue Road still stands.

ARDWOLD
John Craig Eaton

Sir John Craig Eaton's Ardwold, from the east, along the crest of the Davenport ridge.
"On the edge of the hill is the balcony pergola of Corinthian pillars with stone seats and a charming crescent-shaped pool fringed with Verbena and Heliotrope,"
effused Canadian Homes and Gardens *in 1928.* MTRL T11209

John Craig Eaton, born April 28, 1876, was the third son of Timothy Eaton. Edward, the eldest, was groomed for the T. Eaton Company presidency, but he died in 1900 of diabetes. The second son was a maverick, so it was John who rose through the ranks and was promoted to President when Timothy died in 1907.

John had married Flora McCrae in 1901, and the young couple lived first on Walmer Road. John had actually grown up in the Eaton home on Lowther and had roamed through the woods of the Davenport escarpment as a child. As President, he needed a larger home with grounds for entertaining.

John knew Albert Austin of Spadina, as they were both directors of the Dominion Bank. In 1908, John and Flora bought Ravenswood

from Albert's sister, Anne Arthurs. Its neighbours were Glen Edyth and Spadina. As Lady Eaton later wrote in her memoirs:

> All three were spacious semi-country estates, with no crowding of streets nearby, for between Davenport Road and Dupont Street and, again, north to St. Clair there were practically no houses at that time. I would have been happy to move into Mrs. Arthurs' quite charming house, but Jack felt that this was the time to build the sort of place he wanted, and so the two of us began conferences with Frank Wickson of the architectural firm of Wickson & Gregg.

The result was an enormous residence with fifty rooms, fourteen baths, and a half-acre glassed area housing a swimming pool and a conservatory. Construction proceeded swiftly, and often, because of

Ardwold's Music Room around 1922.
Sir John died that year and Lady Eaton left Ardwold for Europe
and later Eaton Hall in King. The Eaton Collection. AO 3740

"The Great Hall with its mechanical organ, circa 1922.
The Eaton Collection. AO 3741

late additions or alterations, the planning was only one floor ahead of the builders.

The Eatons named their home Ardwold, which means "high green hill" in Gaelic. It was a home indeed befitting the head of the largest retail business in the world. The architect, looking out over the city from the escarpment property remarked to Eaton, "Not only have you a splendid view — but imagine being able to look out at four hundred and fifty thousand people who work for you" — an excusable exaggeration.

Ardwold was completed in 1911 while Mrs. Eaton and the children were away on a holiday. Meaning to surprise the family, John had all of the belongings at Walmer moved in during their absence. It was disconcerting enough for Mrs. Eaton, but on being introduced to his new home, their son John David wailed, "I don't like this hotel … I want to go home!"

The entrance to Ardwold was from Spadina Road, and the drive has since become Ardwold Gate. Formal gardens with a fountain pool framed a panoramic view of Toronto. The Great Hall housed a magnificent mechanical organ, which John enjoyed playing most evenings. From a glassed third-floor cupola, the family could take in sunsets and watch the spectacle of Casa Loma rising to the west. There were also a billiards room, a library, a music room, a lounge, a five-room nursery suite with a kitchen, and a private hospital. The hospital was used mostly as a quarantine facility, but three operations were performed there as well. The Eatons enjoyed music parties and riding, and they entertained continuously, especially during the war.

When war broke out, John decided that Eatons would continue to pay full wages to any married man who enlisted, and half pay to single employees. At his own expense, he also outfitted and sent overseas the Eaton Machine Gun Battery. There were endless benefits and fundraisers at Ardwold. In 1915, Eatons sent a trainload of relief supplies to the victims of the Halifax explosion, and John escorted the shipment to distribute goods personally. On June 3, 1915, for his many contributions to the war effort, John Craig Eaton was knighted.

Following the war, Sir John often invited returned soldiers to Ardwold for evenings of music. He was a generous philanthropist, contributing to the T. Eaton Memorial Wing at Toronto Hospital, Timothy Eaton Memorial Church, the Department of Medicine at the University of Toronto, the YMCA, the Royal Ontario Museum, the Navy League, and many other charities. He also worked continually for better working conditions for his employees, introducing shorter hours, minimum wage, early closings, and Saturday half days. He was decisive, big hearted, genuine, and a truly public-spirited man.

In August 1922, Sir John died at forty-six years of age from complications caused by influenza. A hundred thousand people turned out on the day of his funeral to honour the most universally admired philanthropist Toronto has ever known. Lady Eaton decided to live abroad, closer to European schools for her children. As she put it, "To stay at Ardwold was to remind ourselves daily of the loss we had sustained…." Later, Lady Eaton moved to Eaton Hall, in King Township. In 1936, the Toronto property was divided and sold. The house on the high green hill was demolished and Ardwold Gate was developed in its place.

CASA LOMA
Henry Pellatt

Henry Mill Pellatt was probably Toronto's most colourful citizen in his day, and his estate, now owned by the city, is one of the city's stellar attractions.

Henry Pellatt was born in 1859, the eldest son of a stockbroker. He entered his father's business as a clerk at fifteen years of age. In 1876, he began a lifelong association with the Queen's Own Rifles when he enlisted as a rifleman. Pellatt was also an internationally known mile racer, winning the American mile race championship in New York City in 1879. In 1882, he retired from racing, went into the brokerage business full time, and married his neighbourhood sweetheart, Mary Dodgson.

Pellatt became wealthy buying shares in North West Land Company just as Canada's western provinces were beginning to boom. He parlayed those profits into great wealth by investing in hydroelectric power. In 1902, Pellatt was knighted for his work in organizing a number of power companies and bringing the first electricity from Niagara to Toronto.

In April 1903, Pellatt bought twenty-five of the lots James Austin had severed on the west side of Spadina Road. He added to the property two years later by purchasing part of Davenport from Nina de Pencier, thus extending his twenty-five-acre property from Spadina almost to Bathurst. The name Casa Loma is Spanish for "house on the hill."

The Pellatts began building a summer cottage, stables, and greenhouses; the summerhouse was ready for occupation by 1906. Even at this early stage, Sir Henry's grand design was apparent. The stables, which cost nearly $200,000 to erect, had burgundy carpet, imported Spanish-tile flooring, mahogany stalls, and a name plate for each horse engraved in 18-karat gold.

Pellatt hired architect E. J. Lennox, who developed designs based on his own sketches of European castles. Work on the house began in 1910. That same year, Pellatt took his regiment of 750 men to army manoeuvres in Aldershot, England, at his own expense.

Work on Casa Loma proceeded slowly. One of its showpieces was the palm room, with its stained-glass dome. The room was completely finished in marble, with raised beds fitted with steam pipes to keep exotic plants warm during the winter. The massive bronze doors cost $10,000 per pair. Casa Loma also had twenty-five fireplaces, a dining room that could seat a hundred guests, and a Great Hall with an open gallery and seventy-foot ceilings. The furnishings were correspondingly lavish. In the Great Hall, the Pellatts placed a copy of the Coronation Throne at Westminster. Sir Henry's en-suite bath had gold-plated fittings. With a greenhouse, gardens and a deer park, Casa Loma's unabashed ostentation gave Toronto residents plenty to talk about. Its ninety-eight rooms make it one of the largest homes ever built in North America.

Sir Henry maintained his military involvement, eventually being promoted to Major-General

Henry Mill Pellatt (1859–1939) some time during the 1890s.
Sir Henry was knighted in 1902 for his significant contribution to bringing electricity to Toronto. MTRL T30767

Casa Loma during the winter, 1914.
The thoroughbreds pulling the sleigh have been dragged from the comfort of their mahogany stalls with Spanish-tile floors. CTA James 4085

in 1921. It was said that he had the basement at Casa Loma made large enough to drill a battalion. With the hope that Casa Loma might one day become a military museum, Pellatt installed reinforced steel in the floors to support future artillery displays.

The Pellatts moved into Casa Loma in 1913, before it was complete. Toronto was already spreading out, and as the suburbs encroached, taxes rose. Where property taxes had been $600 per year in 1914, they rose to $1,000 per month in the 1920s. Forty staff members incurred an annual payroll expense of $22,000. Lady Eaton described Sir Henry's growing realization that Casa Loma's completion was beyond reach:

> One time Sir Henry took me on a tour of the castle, and I realize now that this was an experience to be treasured — for how often does it happen that one is invited to peer into another person's all-consuming dream? For him that castle was more than life itself; certainly it was obvious to me following him around, up the twisting stone stairs, into the turrets, through the empty, echoing bedrooms…. When our tour was almost over and we were pausing in the corridor before a handsome carved oval frame that was still waiting for a painting, he said, "I wish I had another million dollars. What do you think I would do with it?" There was hardly time for me to answer before he went on, "I'd finish this house — and then I'd die happy."

Lady Pellatt, who had been ill for some time, died in 1923. Just as maintenance expenses became prohibitive, Pellatt's finances faltered; the bank he was involved with collapsed. In 1923, Sir Henry was forced to abandon Casa Loma and sell the contents. Following a five-day auction in June 1924, it was discovered that many of the "priceless" treasures the Pellatts had collected in Europe were nothing more than expensive fakes.

William Sparling took on Casa Loma and tried to run a luxury hotel there between 1925 and 1929, but the venture went bankrupt. In 1934, the city seized Casa Loma for back taxes. A scheme to house the Dionne Quintuplets at the castle on the hill was defeated at city council, so Casa Loma stood vacant for a time. In 1937, the Kiwanis Club leased the property and opened the castle as a tourist attraction. It is still in operation today.

The Second World War provided an interesting but little-known chapter in Casa Loma's history. Under the direction of engineer William Corman, top-secret sonar devices were assembled in the stables that were closed to the public, allegedly for repairs. Parts were covertly brought in on bread wagons and catering supply trucks. Many of the sonar detectors, transmitters, and receiving sets that eventually helped win the war in the Atlantic for the Allies were produced with only a padlock for security, while a thousand visitors a day went through the tourist attraction.

Pellatt remarried, but he died in March 1939 and was buried with military honours. During prosperous times he had amassed $17 million. But by the time of his death, his assets had dwindled to $35,000.

ROSEDALE
William Botsford Jarvis

William Botsford Jarvis's Rosedale was part of the original two-hundred-acre farm granted to Captain George Playter in 1796. In 1821, John Small had bought the western part of the lot. Three years later, Small sold the enlarged 120-acre property to William Botsford Jarvis.

William's father, Colonel Stephen Jarvis, was a cousin of Secretary William Jarvis, making Samuel Peters Jarvis of Hazelburn and William Botsford second cousins. After William's mother died in 1819, his brother and sister moved away, so he and his father lived bachelors' lives on the former Small property.

In May 1827, William Botsford was appointed High Sheriff of the Home District, and two months later he married William Dummer Powell's granddaughter Mary Boyles Powell. Sheriff Jarvis was an energetic and well-liked young man. The Chief Justice congratulated his granddaughter upon her choice, saying, " I had occasion for no very intimate acquaintance with Mr. Jarvis, but have always thought him to be a prudent and well disposed character, the more likely to ensure happiness in the married state."

Mary Jarvis named the estate for the wild roses that bloomed on the property. The approach to Rosedale entered from Yonge Street, crossed a primitive bridge over the ravine, and climbed steeply to the house.

As the family grew to include five children, the Jarvises expanded

the farmhouse. John Howard drew the plans for two new wings in 1835. They accommodated a morning room, a large verandah, a grape house, a peach house, a conservatory, and additional bedrooms. The elegant residence was surrounded by gardens where paths wound through orchards, quiet arbours, rose gardens, and masses of flowers. About this time, William and Joseph Bloor subdivided the land between the ravine and modern Bedford Drive and laid out the village of Yorkville. Jarvis also opened a new approach for Rosedale along modern Roxborough Street, planting the boulevards with trees.

Sheriff Jarvis was a hero in York for defending the town in 1837. He led an outpost guard that turned back the rebels to Montgomery's Tavern. Mary was at Rosedale with two seriously ill children. At the last moment, she took the family by carriage behind Rosedale, down through Moss Park, and into town. Rosedale was spared.

The family moved away for a number of years while the children were educated. In 1853, Jarvis sold most of the estate to a developer, who registered a plan that divided a hundred acres into sixty-two lots and laid out a number of curving streets — Avondale, Rosedale, Crescent, South Drive, and Park Road. A practical solution to the challenge of the ravine, the curvilinear design was one of the first in North America. The subdivision was called Rose Park. Edgar Jarvis, a nephew, also had a hand in the development of the

William Botsford Jarvis (1799–1864). Jarvis sat for this photo with his two sons, William and Colborne, in the early 1860s. By that time, a developer had laid out most of the Jarvis estate as Rose Park subdivision, one of the first subdivisions in North America with curving streets. MTRL T13717

William and Mary Jarvis's Rosedale, circa 1835. This drawing by James Hamilton shows the two wings designed by John Howard. The house stood on the west side of what became Rosedale Road, just south of Cluny Avenue. MTRL JRR T30696

new garden suburb. He built many fine homes in the area, but a depression between 1854 and 1865, and the remote location, slowed sales. Jarvis reserved the Rosedale house and twenty acres, and his three married daughters and their husbands lived there after Mary died in 1854.

William died at Rosedale in 1864, and the remaining estate was subdivided and sold. David Macpherson, on neighbouring Chestnut Park, added the Rosedale homestead to his estate. In 1905, the house was demolished as Cluny Drive was put through.

From Sheriff Jarvis's farm grew a park-like suburb that eventually drew Toronto's elite from Jarvis and Sherbourne Streets. Rosedale became the preserve of the well-to-do, the tree-lined streets and winding ways harking back to the happy country life enjoyed at the Jarvis home.

DRUMSNAB
Francis Cayley / Maunsell B. Jackson

In 1834, Francis Cayley bought the eastern part of George Playter's farm lot, including the Playter house. Cayley named the property for a round hill in the Don Valley that he could see from the house. The hill resembled a sugar loaf, or a *drumsnab*, in the dialect of England's north country. Cayley was a self-taught artist and architect, and he set about enlarging the Playter house, parts of which dated back to 1808.

Drumsnab was surrounded by a wild landscape, and Cayley's Regency design — with French doors and verandahs — took advantage of the natural surroundings. In *Toronto of Old*, Henry Scadding quoted an 1849 observer:

> The most picturesque spot near Toronto and within four miles of it is Drumsnab, the residence of Mr. Cayley. The mansion is roomy and of one storey, with a broad verandah. It is seated among fields and woods, on the edge of a slope; at the bottom winds a river; opposite is a most singular conical hill, like an immense Indian tumulus for the dead; in the distance, through a vista cut judiciously through the forest are seen the dark blue waters of Lake Ontario. The walls of the principal room are covered with scenes from Faust, drawn in fresco, with a bold and masterly hand, by the proprietor.

Cayley also rendered Don Quixote on door panels and a trompe l'oeil hatrack, complete with hat, cloak, and stick, in the forty-five-foot-long hall. Drumsnab's walls were thirty inches thick and covered with stucco. The ceilings were twelve feet high, and the wainscoting and balusters were made from trees cut on the property.

By 1850, Cayley's younger brother, John, had married Clara Boulton, a niece of D'Arcy Boulton Jr., and the couple had come to live at Drumsnab. The Cayleys added a second floor and attic. A ballroom with marble mantelpieces spanned the entire south side of the second floor, and several bedrooms with immense windows were also added.

During this period, Cayley began selling off his property. When Francis died in 1874, the remaining property went to his brother. John sold Drumsnab and its acreage to Maunsell B. Jackson three years later. Only eight acres around the house and twenty-six in the valley remained. The rest had become part of the suburb of Rosedale.

Maunsell B. Jackson Jr. wrote:

> Though the house was at that time over 50 years old, I was the first child born in it. I never cared much for the building itself nor did the Frank Cayleys who originally built it as a bungalow. It was a Cayley house, of course; we were merely purchasers. They held that adding the upper storey ruined a beautiful bungalow and didn't make a real house. I agree with them.

In spite of this, Maunsell Jr. and his sister lived at Drumsnab for eighty-eight and ninety years respectively.

In 1914, the Prince Edward Viaduct was built across the Don River, opening east Toronto to development. A piece of the ravine and the Drumsnab property were expropriated, and the Playter lodge

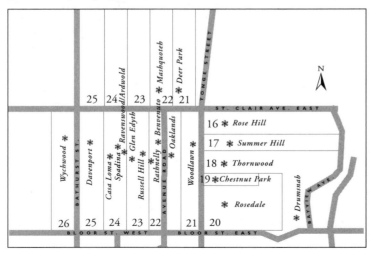

Frances Cayley bought the eastern part of George Playter's farm lot and erected his Drumsnab on the Playter foundations

Drumsnab, circa 1845, a few years before Francis Cayley's brother, John, and his wife, Clara Boulton, moved in.
John and Clara added a second floor and an attic. MTRL T11172

house, which had been Francis Cayley's studio, was demolished. Another portion of the property was expropriated when the ramp to the Don Valley Parkway was built in 1961. Most of the remaining Drumsnab gardens were subdivided in 1965, when a Jackson descendant sold the property.

Drumsnab is said to be the oldest Toronto residence still in use as a private home. Cayley's hatrack mural was discovered beneath wallpaper during restorations in 1967. Under his trompe l'oeil, Cayley had written, "As long as Drumsnab stands my hat and cloak will hang in the front hall." So they do.

Chestnut Park, circa 1900.
Senator David Macpherson's impressive residence was home to St. Andrew's College from 1899 to 1904. MTRL T11413

CHESTNUT PARK
David Macpherson

Chestnut Park, on the east side of Yonge Street, between present-day Roxborough and Rowanwood, was the villa and estate of Senator David Macpherson.

David Macpherson, born near Inverness, Scotland, in 1818, arrived in Upper Canada in 1835. He entered a shipping firm, where his brother was senior partner, but he later went into the railway contracting business with engineer Casimir Gzowski. In 1844, Macpherson married Elizabeth Sarah of the affluent Molson family of Montreal. Macpherson and Gzowski made their fortunes in 1853, with the construction of the Grand Trunk Railway.

Macpherson bought his estate, which was just north of Sheriff Jarvis's Rosedale, from merchant and landowner William Mathers in 1855. Mathers had built the original house, but the Macphersons immediately set about altering it to accommodate their large family. They used the architectural firm of Cumberland and Storm, as the Gzowskis were to do a few years later, and the result was an elegant and impressive residence much like the better-known Gzowski home.

The villa faced Yonge Street, and along that frontage Macpherson had a row of horse chestnuts planted. The brick house was situated in a grove of trees, while well-kept lawns — graced with planters and statues — and farmlands lay to the east. The 1855 additions included a library, a nursery suite, a ground-floor school room, and additional bedchambers, bringing the total to seven bedrooms. The drawing room was enlarged to twenty-two by thirty feet, and intricate ornamentation was added, with mantelpieces, newel posts, window frames, and other interior trim. The family of nine hosted numerous social functions.

In 1864, Macpherson embarked on his political career, winning a seat on the Legislative Council of Canada. Three years later, he was among the first appointees to the Canadian Senate, and in 1880 he was made Speaker of the Senate. David Macpherson was knighted while serving as Minister of the Interior in Sir John A. Macdonald's government between 1883 and 1885. He retired from politics in 1885 due to ill health and criticism over his handling of the Northwest Rebellion.

When the Rosedale estate was subdivided, Macpherson bought the old Jarvis house. His daughter Christina and her husband, Percival Ridout, lived there from 1889 to 1905. After Macpherson's death in 1896, the family sold the entire estate to developers. St. Andrews College occupied the Chestnut Park house from 1899 to 1904. After the college moved to their campus north of the city, the house was demolished.

Architect S. H. Townsend laid out the Chestnut Park subdivision with winding streets and several deluxe features — brick sidewalks, paved streets, telephone and gas service to the rear, and posh streetlamps. Townsend designed street widths that allowed two carriages to pass while a third was parked at the curb, but the streets were narrower than many being built at the time. An article that appeared in *The Canadian Architect and Builder* in 1905 explained, "Automobile speeding is not desirable in a residential district and the roads need not be designed to suit its requirements." The first bids for building contracts were opened in 1902, and additional lots were severed in 1905. The exclusive area was promoted as North Rosedale, and most of the large homes were sold before or during construction. Houses were set back according to the topography, which resulted in pleasant boulevards, pretty stone retaining walls, and graceful corners. Chestnut Park and Macpherson Avenue remind us of the earlier estate.

THORNWOOD
Joseph Price

Price's Mill, on Price's Creek, during the early 1840s. The mill stood at the intersection of today's Roxborough Drive and Mount Pleasant Road. Part of the Price estate was purchased later by David Macpherson for Chestnut Park.
MTRL JRR T10893

Joseph Price and his daughter Sarah lived on a sizeable piece of property east of Yonge Street that extended from today's Rowanwood Avenue to the railway tracks. It was a large estate, and Prices lived there for most of the 1800s, but not much is known about them or their home.

Price was born near Hertford, England, in 1790. He lived in New York for a time, where he worked in the brass and iron trade, and came to Canada in 1814 after the war. He lived a number of places in and around York, finally purchasing lot 18, in the second concession from the Elmsley estate. The property reached eastward to the Don River, and a creek bisected the lot close to the intersection of today's Mount Pleasant Road and Roxborough Street East. Price named the property after his birthplace. The family home was a large, red-brick, L-shaped residence.

Thornwood supported a working farm, but it was also heavily treed. Price went into lumbering and built a sawmill on the creek, which was subsequently named for him. Joseph married Maria Kimberly, and they had two sons and a daughter. He was a member of the Church of England, a Freemason, and a Conservative in politics. Not surprisingly, then, he served with the militia during the 1837 uprising and was made a captain.

Joseph died in 1846. Part of his land was sold to merchant William Mathers, who subsequently sold the southwest portion to David Macpherson of Chestnut Park. Price left ten acres fronting on Yonge Street to his only daughter, Sarah. Sarah never married and she lived in a modest one-and-a-half-storey roughcast cottage closer to Yonge Street. By the 1870s, two streets occupying most of the Yonge Street frontage, Price and Grimsby, were opened and laid out with small lots for working-class housing. In 1883, when the Village of Yorkville was annexed, Miss Price's north lot line marked the northern

city limits. There was still a lumberyard on the lot in 1890.

By 1897, Sarah had moved to Spadina Road, although she still owned several lots on Yonge Street that were used as homes and offices and provided her with rental income. In 1905, while Sarah retained ownership of a number of Yonge Street properties, the strip had become increasingly commercial, as companies including Elias Rogers Coal and Wood and the CPR purchased frontage.

In 1912, impatient with construction delays at the new Union Station, the CPR decided to open a passenger station on the former Price property to serve its cross-town line just south of the escarpment. A second, more impressive stone station was opened in June 1916 and was in use until 1929. This familiar landmark was leased shortly afterward to the Liquor Control Board of Ontario.

Visitors to the former North Toronto Station will notice several streets in the area with Price roots: Price Street, Pricefield Road, and Thornwood Road.

Yonge Street in 1905. Sarah Price still owned a number of properties along this stretch of Yonge at the time, although the house in the foreground belonged to Lydia Trump. To the south, with the great stack of wood, was the Elias Rogers Coal and Wood Company.
CTA DPW14 Vol. 5 72

William Larratt Smith's Summer Hill, circa 1900. The estate was named by its earlier owner, Charles Thompson, who opened his house and grounds as an amusement area — Summer Hill Spring Park and Pleasure Grounds — when rail transport took its toll on his stagecoach business. MTRL T11521

SUMMER HILL
Charles Thompson / Larratt Smith

Lot 17, in the second concession, was granted first to John Playter, but by 1831 he had moved to the east side of the Don River. In 1842, the new owner of the two-hundred-acre lot east of Yonge street started to plan his home. Architect John Howard drew "plans, specifications and estimates for a brick villa on the east side of Yonge Street for Charles Thompson, Esq."

Thompson ran stagecoaches and steamboats for passengers and later for freight and mail delivery. He is best known for his stagecoach business on Yonge Street. Thompson's new house stood just off Yonge, atop a hill facing west, "commanding," as Henry Scadding put it, "a noble view of the wide plain below, including Toronto with its spires and the lake view along the horizon…."

By 1853, rail transportation was taking its toll on Thompson's coach business, so he sold off portions of his estate and opened a summer amusement park overlooking the ravine. It was a favourite destination for day trips and picnics, and Thompson's drawing room became a dance hall — a most popular attraction. Thompson named his amusement area Summer Hill Spring Park and Pleasure Grounds. The road into the park was called Thompson Avenue (now Summerhill Avenue), while Shaftesbury Avenue to the south was called Charles Street in those days.

By 1866, the Summer Hill property had dwindled to seventy-five acres. That year, lawyer and businessman Larratt William Smith purchased the Summer Hill house and estate. Smith had come to York as a boy with his family

in 1832. He studied law and then articled in William Henry Draper's offices. Draper, who later became Chief Justice, was a member of the city's privileged class, and he and Mrs. Draper introduced Smith into Toronto society as their protégé. Smith went on to become a director of a number of companies and president of the Consumers Gas Company, amassing considerable personal wealth.

With his second wife, Mary, Larratt turned Summer Hill into a grand residence. The dance hall was restored to a drawing room, this time with its sixty-by-thirty-foot expanse covered with an immense Persian carpet. The Smith family grew to include five sons and three daughters, which called for additional rooms at Summer Hill, bringing the total to thirty-five. The coach house and stables were built of brick. East of the house, fifty acres were planted in orchards and vineyards, while the gardens and lawns close to the house were considered among the finest in the city. Smith was a lover of birds, which flocked to this green retreat, and he forbade any hunting on the property. His children enjoyed rambles in the ravine, just as the pleasure-seekers of a previous generation had.

The area was annexed to the city in 1903. Smith died two years later. By 1913, Joseph Vaughan (a brother of J. J. Vaughan of Donningvale) had bought Summer Hill, subdivided it for small houses and apartments, and sold off the lots. Mount Pleasant Road ran through the former pleasure grounds. Only the coach house on Summerhill Gardens remains, but the whole district still bears the name Summerhill.

Mary Elizabeth and Larratt William Violett Smith.
Under the Smiths, Summer Hill was turned into a grand residence. MTRL T13792

The Elms, circa 1900. The house was originally built by Walter and Anna (nee Ketchum) Rose and named Rose Hill. MTRL T31795

ROSE HILL
Walter and Anna Rose / Joseph Jackes

Before it was purchased by Jesse Ketchum, lot 16, in the second concession, immediately south of St. Clair, was held by a number of owners, including Duncan Cameron of Gore Vale and William Allan of Moss Park. The wealthy tanner and philanthropist presented the two-hundred-acre lot to his daughter Anna and her husband, Walter Rose, in the late 1830s. Rose and Ketchum were also business partners in a private banking venture. The house, which stood just north of today's Jackes Avenue, back from Yonge Street, had a centre hall and verandah and was built of red brick. The stables were to the north, while oak forest and fields stretched east to modern Bayview Avenue. Unfortunately, Anna died only a few years later.

An elm on the property had a perfectly horizontal branch, and apocryphal rumours persisted for years that rebels were hanged here after the 1837 Rebellion. It is thought that this is what prompted the name long applied to this stretch of Yonge Street — Gallows Hill.

After Walter Rose died, the Rose Hill property was divided and sold. In 1865, Joseph Jackes, of the Castlefield family, bought the house and the surrounding property that extended from today's Woodlawn to just south of Rosehill Avenue. He wrote to his brother, "I shall soon have as nice a place as there is on Yonge Street. I have the best situation about Toronto, a fine orchard, splendid view, capital house, tip-top pony and buggy, a number one wife...." Joseph and Emma had a large number of children, and Joseph travelled to his law offices in Toronto each day, while his children grew up in the country.

The Jackes had renovations done to the house, converting a basement kitchen into a billiard room. Joseph and Emma renamed the estate The Elms, and they improved the orchard by adding plum, peach, and pear trees. In 1874, Joseph wrote to his brother:

My home is a large red brick house at the top of a hill, vulgarly known as Gallows Hill, on the right hand side going north. I bought it cheap and have improved it greatly, so that now, with the improvements and the increase in property, it has become worth about $20,000.

In 1872, the city acquired a large section of The Elms for a reservoir. A subdivision plan for twenty-four lots was drawn up in 1884. A few of the lots along the south side of St. Clair were purchased right away.

One of these purchasers was John Thomas Moore, a chartered accountant and developer. Moore was managing director of the Toronto Belt Line Railway, the commuter railway designed to serve Toronto's suburbs in the boom years of the late 1880s. Moore envisioned a park-like residential district around the St. Clair East area and he filed his first plan for Glenrose Avenue west of Clifton Road in 1889. His residence, Avoca Villa, stood at the corner of modern Inglewood and Rose Park Drives. Moore was famous for his love of roses; he founded the Rose Society of Toronto and imported shrubs for his garden from Great Britain. The depression of 1893 and ensuing real estate slump caused the Belt Line's failure in 1894. Moore's plan for a garden subdivision failed too, but the neighbourhood that grew up in the area following the First World War was eventually named for him.

Emma Jackes died in 1886, and Joseph in 1898. A son, Edwin, his wife, Emily, and a sister lived on at The Elms until Edwin died in 1930.

The area surrounding the house became increasingly commercial and taxes rose steeply. For a time, The Elms housed the offices of a used-car dealership. Then, after lying vacant for a number of years, it was demolished in 1948 to make way for apartment buildings. Jackes, Avoca, and Rosehill Avenues remain.

Moore Place around 1878, several years after Charles Moore's death.
From the *Illustrated Historical Atlas of the County of York* (1878). MTRL T11424

MOORE PLACE
Charles Moore

Most of the properties in the third concession were farms right up until subdivision, rather than country estates. Interesting exceptions were lots 16, 17, and 19.

Lot 19 was the only two-hundred-acre farm still intact when it was purchased from the Cawthra family in 1873. In the early years, non-residents who died in Toronto and citizens who did not belong to the Anglican Church were buried at Potters Field, in Yorkville. By the mid-1800s, the cemetery was crowded. The Toronto Burial Grounds trustees, led by William McMaster, purchased the two hundred acres, with a quarter-mile frontage on Yonge Street, and had Mount Pleasant Cemetery designed by H. A. Englehart. Originally, the park-like burial ground had ponds, cascades, ducks, swans, and lush plantings.

The other large lot reserved from development was the clergy reserve on lot 17. Augustus George Dinnick developed his Glebe Estates here after the First World War, laying out streets including Manor Road and Belsize Drive.

Immediately north of the clergy reserve was lot 16, originally granted to Rev. Thomas Raddish. In 1832, Charles Moore bought the property, which ran east from Yonge south of modern Eglinton Avenue, from intervening owners.

Moore was born in Ireland in 1793. With his wife, Eleanor, and an infant son, he immigrated to New York prior to the war. Charles was a staunch Loyalist, so he found a warm welcome when war necessitated a move to Queenston. There the Moores lived a pioneer existence in the bush before moving to York County in 1823. A daughter Catherine was actually born en route. The family farmed on rented property for a time before purchasing the property they dubbed Moore Place, for £250, in 1832.

With five sons and three daughters in the family, Moore Place was at the centre of a busy household that relied on farming for its livelihood. The house faced Yonge Street and was surrounded by tidy lawns and gardens. The Moores prospered and were able to summer in Muskoka in later years.

The family was well connected with the conservative ruling class of Toronto. Charles served in the militia and opposed Mackenzie's rebellion, even though he could see Montgomery's Tavern from his second-floor window. Moore was also a personal friend of Bishop Strachan, who would break up his periodic trips to preach at St. John's Church in York Mills with an overnight stay at the Moore home.

In 1860, Charles Moore sold the rear portion of the estate, near today's Bayview Avenue, to his son, Erwin, but Charles held on to the 135 acres closest to Yonge, which he willed to his daughters. He died in 1867. His widow continued to live at Moore Place with the daughters, even as they began selling off acreage. Eleanor died in 1875.

Mary and Catherine Moore, unable to manage the large farm, sold the property north of today's Soudan Avenue for $4,000. Developers purchased it subsequently for $55,000. Alfred Lambe and Robert Petman developed the area as fourteen short residential streets running north from Soudan.

In 1889, the two sisters moved to the city to be closer to St. Paul's Church in Yorkville, a parish that the Moore family had helped to found in 1842. Thomas Moore, a nephew, lived at the old homestead with his family for a number of years before its demolition. No trace remains today of Moore Place.

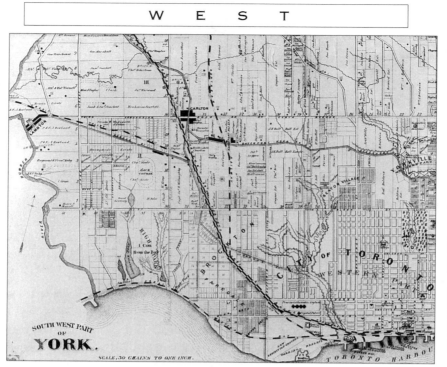

The Map of the South West Part of York *shows many of the larger estates:*
the Gwynne estate, John Henry Dunn's property, High Park, and John Ellis's Herne Hill.
From the *Illustrated Historical Atlas of the County of York* (1878),

WEST LODGE
Walter O'Hara

Parkdale was once covered in a mature forest of oak, hickory, butternut, walnut, white pine, and basswood. Occupying high ground west of the growing city, the district afforded panoramic views of Lake Ontario. Colonel Walter O'Hara was one of the first property owners in that part of York Township.

O'Hara was born in Dublin in 1789. He graduated from Trinity College, where he had studied law, and then entered the military. Walter distinguished himself between 1808 and 1815 for his part in the Napoleonic Wars. He fought in all of the major battles in Spain, including Roncesvalles and Sorauren, was twice wounded, and was decorated with several medals and honours.

In 1826, O'Hara immigrated to Upper Canada with his wife, Marian Murray, and was appointed Assistant Adjutant General of the Militia of Upper Canada. Colonel O'Hara was known for his good sense and leadership. Wrote Henry Scadding, "His contemporaries will always think of him as a chivalrous, high-spirited, warm-hearted gentleman."

In 1831 the O'Haras bought park lot 31. On the hundred acres, O'Hara established a farm and built his home, West Lodge, named after his family's residence in Ireland. West Lodge was a solid and attractive red-brick Georgian home that must have accommodated the O'Haras, with their three sons and five daughters, very

West Lodge stood north of Queen Street at what is now West Lodge Avenue. This view of Colonel O'Hara's home is taken from a watercolour by Robert O'Hara. MTRL JRR T11429

comfortably. In 1840, Colonel O'Hara purchased lots 33 and 34, to the west, adding another 420 acres to his land holdings. The *Cyclopaedia of Canadian Biography* records, "Colonel O'Hara and Mr. Spragge were the first settlers in that part of the township of York now known as the town of Parkdale, and there he erected a residence and formed what was for many years an oasis in a grand forest."

O'Hara was known for his determination and high principles. When his superior's vacant position was filled through patronage, O'Hara petitioned unsuccessfully and was forced to retire in 1846. The colonel was bitter, and he remained critical of the narrow Canadian political scene. He withdrew to West Lodge, where he adopted the life of a country squire.

In 1856, O'Hara subdivided lots 33 and 34, creating thirteen villa lots with Lake Shore Road frontage. He named Sorauren and Roncesvalles Avenues for two of the battles he fought under the Duke of Wellington. Next, he subdivided the north part of the park lot, preserving the portion south of the rail lines surrounding West Lodge. In 1868, O'Hara further subdivided the 1856 villa lots into seventy-six lots of between two and fourteen acres. Roland and Alhambra Streets were opened at that time.

Colonel O'Hara died in 1874. The following year his wife sold most of the remaining park lot property to the Toronto House Building Association. The association opened West Lodge and O'Hara Avenues and laid out ninety-six building lots.

The O'Hara house went to the Congregation of Our Lady of Charity of the Good Shepherd, where the nuns opened a reformatory for "fallen" women. From 1898 to 1941, West Lodge housed a girls' reform school — St. Euphrasia's. The Sisters of the Good Shepherd moved to larger premises in 1956, and the city purchased and demolished the building before seniors' apartments were built on the site in 1960.

A map of the area shows O'Hara's hand in the subdivision of his property. Marion Street was named for Mrs. O'Hara, and Fermanagh Avenue for the Irish county where the Colonel was born. Walter (now Grenadier Road), Geoffrey, Constance, and Ruth (now Fern Avenue) Streets were named for his children.

Lieutenant-Colonel Walter O'Hara (1789–1874) at eighty-two years of age. O'Hara fought in all of the major battles in Spain during the Peninsular Wars against Napoleon. He named Roncesvalles and Sorauren Avenues after two of those campaigns. MTRL JRR T32039

ELM GROVE
William Charles Gwynne

William Charles Gwynne was born in Castleknock, Ireland, in 1806. He studied medicine at Trinity College, Dublin, and came to Canada as a ship's surgeon in 1832. He quickly established a respectable practice in York. Dr. Gwynne acquired nearly 115 acres in the eastern part of broken front lot 31, which was south of present Queen and west of Dufferin, running down to the lake. In 1835, Dr. Gwynne married Anne Murray Powell, sister of Mrs. William Botsford Jarvis and granddaughter of William Dummer Powell. The Gwynnes had John Howard build a large home for them, in 1836, on what is now the west side of Dufferin, between Temple and Thorburn. They named their house, nestled as it was in a stand of trees, Elm Grove.

Contemporaries described the Gwynne home as a picturesque cottage with an eighteen-foot-wide hall and nearly two-foot-thick walls. Some of the joists were forty feet long, and the mortar walls were reinforced to half height with iron plates. Inside were seven rooms, including a large parlour. French doors looked out over the lawn and down to the lake. A large copper bell, presented to Charles when he left his Irish home, was installed at Elm Grove and was used to summon the farm labourers to meals.

Gwynne was a vocal critic of the Tory-managed medical institutions of the time and, after reforms, he took his place on the Medical Board of Upper Canada in 1838. In 1842, he was also appointed a professor at King's College. John Ross Robertson described Gwynne as "an earnest and energetic man in everything relating to his profession. He could not tolerate half-heartedness, and he strove to imbue his pupils at the University with a like energy."

In 1853, as a result of a politically motivated decision, the University's medical department was disbanded, and an irate Gwynne sailed for England. In Britain, he was manager of a railway construction firm. He also oversaw the construction of the Thames Embankment in London.

But Gwynne was back in Toronto three years later, reassuming his position on the medical board and devoting a greater portion of his time to farming and entomology. He lost a great deal of money when the Toronto, Grey and Bruce Railway failed to repay an advance he had made, and thereafter, he was plagued with mortgages and debts. He sold a few small lots and took a position as manager of the Toronto House Building Association. The association developed and promoted Parkdale as a fashionable suburb for Toronto's business and professional families.

Gwynne died of an ulcer in 1875, leaving a daughter and, as the *Dictionary of Canadian Biography* described her, a "shrewish wife." Three sons predeceased their father. Gwynne's family divided the northern thirty acres of Elm Grove into suburban villa lots. The Toronto House Building Association bought all six lots and further subdivided them into twenty-eight, laying out Greig, Gwynne, and Melbourne Avenues. Greig was originally named for the president of the House Building Association, but was later changed to Elm Grove Avenue.

In 1877, the middle third of the property between King and the railway, was subdivided. Gwynne's daughter, Nell, named Huxley, Tyndall, and Spencer Streets after the natural philosophers her

William Charles Gwynne (1806–1875). A member of the Medical Board of Upper Canada and a professor at King's College, Gwynne was later involved in land development both in England and Toronto. From The Medical Profession in Upper Canada.

Gwynne's home, Elm Grove, circa 1895, after much of the estate had been subdivided. Gwynne's daughter lived in the house — which stood on the west side of Dufferin, between Thorburn and Temple Avenues — until 1910.

father had so admired. She retained the block around Elm Grove. The area south of the tracks was laid out as residential streets as well, but the city bought the lakefront properties to enlarge the exhibition grounds. Most of the estate, as part of the Village of Parkdale, was annexed in 1889.

Nell never married. From her bedroom window, she could look out at an ancient elm known locally as the trysting tree. By carefully preserving this tree on her property, Miss Gwynne perpetuated a local story about a lost fiancé.

Nell died at Elm Grove in 1910. The property was sold off by her executors, and the house was demolished in 1917 to make way for apartments.

COLBORNE LODGE
John George Howard

John Corby was born near London in 1803. At the age of fourteen, he joined the Navy, where he was trained in surveying and drafting. In 1827, he married Jemima Meikle. Five years later, the couple decided to pursue a new life in Upper Canada. Before emigrating, John re-adopted the old family name of Howard and added a George for good measure — in deference to family patriarch, George Howard, the Sixth Earl of Carlisle.

Jemima and John had an eventful passage from Britain. Howard missed the ship twice and was almost knocked overboard when the boom caught him on the side of the head. He narrowly escaped being lost at sea on a fishing excursion and returned to the ship only to endure mutiny, shipwreck, and a cholera outbreak.

Fortuitously, when the Howards arrived in Canada, Lieutenant-Governor John Colborne was searching for a drawing master for Upper Canada College. Howard taught during the mornings and then devoted afternoons to his professional work — architecture, surveying, and engineering. Howard's fortunes were assured with his appointment as city surveyor in 1834. In that post, he designed all sorts of projects, from King Street sewers to Toronto's third jail. His most ambitious work was the Provincial Lunatic Asylum on Queen Street. He also drew plans for dozens of private residences, including

Dundonald, Moss Park, Woodlawn, Mashquoteh, Rosedale, Summer Hill, and Elm Grove. Wrote McRae and Adamson in *The Ancestral Roof*, "A designer, architect and engineer, he tried out anything new that appealed to his love of experiment." Jemima provided very real assistance, aiding on the surveys and scrupulously copying specifications.

In 1836, Howard bought lot 37, in the first concession, from King's College (lots 36, 37, and 38 had been granted to the college by the Crown). The Howards named their home Colborne Lodge in honour of their benefactor. They moved into the Regency-style villa in December 1837. The Howards made several later additions, including the bathroom, which was one of the first in the city with running water.

Since the 165-acre estate occupied the highest point in the area, Howard named it High Park. Too busy to farm the property, he brought in a tenant farmer in 1851. A staff of three served the comfortable household and maintained the landscaped grounds. On the front lawn, Howard mounted a naval gun, which he fired every dawn and dusk. He also maintained a beacon to aid navigation on Lake Ontario. On a more whimsical note, Howard carved a lifelike dragon from a twisted tree root and placed the glittering-eyed serpent on his verandah railing.

Although John had three children with widow Mary Williams, the Howards never had any children of their own. They decided to give their property to the city, as a park, in 1873. The offer came with two conditions: the Howards would retain the house and surrounding forty-five acres

The Entrance Gate to Colborne Lodge and the High Park estate, circa 1879, from a watercolour by John Howard. The artist would be standing in the middle of today's Gardiner Expressway.
MTRL T11328

John George Howard (1803–1890), an architect and city surveyor, designed everything from King Street sewers and the Provincial Lunatic Asylum on Queen Street West to private residences including Dundonald, Moss Park, Woodlawn, and Mashquoteh. MTRL T32140

Colborne Lodge during the 1920s, around the time the Women's Canadian Historical Society did some restoration and opened the house to the public. MTRL T11333

until their deaths, and John would draw an annual pension of $1200 per year to act as Forest Ranger. Howard was seventy years old; the council agreed.

In 1877, Jemima died following a lengthy illness. John built a massive stone monument and surrounded it with fencing salvaged from St. Paul's Cathedral in London. The fence also had a rough passage; the ship carrying it sank in the St. Lawrence and the wrought iron had to be recovered.

John lived until 1890. Interestingly, Howard's total pension amounted to $20,400; Howard had valued his property at $24,000. The deed to the estate specified that it be called High Park in perpetuity and that no liquor ever be sold there. Two servants lived in the house until 1913, and then it stood vacant until 1925, when the Women's Canadian Historical Society undertook some restoration and opened the house to the public. In 1960, the Toronto Historical Board took over. After extensive restoration work in the late 1960s, the house was reopened in 1970.

The city eventually added land on both sides to bring the park's total to four hundred acres. Howard's influence lives on in the names of High Park, Howard Park Avenue, and Colborne Lodge.

George Cheney's Sunnyside, built by John Howard on speculation.
This picnic, in August 1859, was given by the Toronto Field Battery in honour of Lieutenant Charles Holiwell. MTRL T11175

SUNNYSIDE
John Howard / George Cheney

In 1844, seven years after moving into Colborne Lodge, John Howard entered into real estate speculation on the lot adjoining High Park on the east.

John Howard and Frederick Barron bought lot 35 from the Honourable George Crookshank, former Receiver General and member of the Legislative Council. Barron, from 1843 to 1856, was Principal of Upper Canada College, where John Howard was Drawing Master. The property comprised 160 acres, stretching from Lake Ontario up to modern Bloor, between present-day Sunnyside Avenue and Parkside Drive.

In 1848, Howard bought out Barron and began to divide the property into smaller lots, to be sold either with or without a home. Howard ran advertisements in the *Globe* for "Villas and garden lots, with a fine view of the lake, three miles from St. George's Church."

The first home Howard built for sale on one of these lots was named Sunnyside. The name may have come from Washington Irving's home near Tarrytown, New York. Toronto's Sunnyside was on the north side of modern Queensway, between Sunnyside and Glendale Avenues. At that time, bears and wolves still lived in the woods close by, and Native people continued to travel the long-used trail through the property, which Howard laid out as Indian Road.

Sunnyside was designed in the Regency style that is Howard's trademark, with verandahs, fanciful decoration, tall chimneys, and a stucco finish. He placed the house to take full advantage of its natural setting, and Sunnyside's Gothic windows looked out over the lake. Although Howard had built a basement kitchen, fairly common for the time, in his own home he decided on a main-floor cooking area in this house.

In 1853, Howard sold the house, with just under ten acres, to merchant George H. Cheney for £1,200 over several instalments. Great Western Railway bought its right of way along the lakeshore, at the south end of High Park and Sunnyside, in the following year. Cheney was a stove manufacturer, and although he could afford to buy adjoining property in 1853, his business was bankrupt a short four years later. Sunnyside went to his creditors, and only when Cheney's estate was settled in 1864 did Howard receive payment — just over $1,000. Howard continued to sell off lots, even though road access was still very poor.

The whole district eventually became known as Sunnyside, and in 1888 it was annexed to the city. A boardwalk along the south end of the subdivision was a popular destination for promenades prior to the First World War. Sunnyside also gave its name to the recreational area and amusement park developed on the lakeshore during the war. The first major edifice was the Pavilion Restaurant. The grandiose Sunnyside Bathing Pavilion opened in 1922.

The Sunnyside villa later became Sacred Heart Orphanage, administered by the Sisters of St. Joseph. When the orphanage was threatened by expropriation in 1920, the facility was converted to St. Joseph's Hospital. The villa was demolished in 1945 to make space for a new hospital building, and most of Sunnyside Park was dismantled in the late 1950s to make way for the Gardiner Expressway.

John Ellis's Herne Hill, circa 1880. John Ellis Jr. inherited the Grenadier Heights home after his father's death in 1877.
He severed and sold off the estate, and the house was demolished in 1925. MTRL T30951

HERNE HILL
John Ellis

Lot 38, to the west of Howard's High Park, was another lot originally reserved by the Crown and later granted to King's College. The pond on the property was already known as Grenadiers' Pond by the time John Ellis purchased the property. The name dated back to the War of 1812. A party of British soldiers were on their way across the frozen pond to meet the American troops as they landed, when the ice gave way. Several of the grenadiers drowned.

John Ellis was born in Norfolk, England, in 1795. He married Rhonda Anne Benton and moved to London, where he became a successful businessman. He had two country estates in nearby Essex, but he disposed of his English property and sailed for Canada, probably in the late 1830s. Ellis purchased lot 38 in 1838, and the family lived a rugged pioneer life for the first few years on the heavily forested property. Later he built a brick home — Herne Hill — on the ridge to the west of Grenadier Pond (today's Grenadier Heights) and cleared farmlands.

In 1845, Ellis opened a printing business on King Street west of Yonge and the family's fortunes became secure. Ellis was an expert engraver, although most of his orders were for fairly commonplace stationery — notepaper, announcements, wedding invitations, and calling cards. Some of his bigger projects included the 1858 *Plan of Toronto*. John Jr. joined his father in the engraving business, but in 1868 Ellis sold the business, which went on to become Rolph, Smith and Company, and retired to his Herne Hill estate and farm.

John Ellis was an accomplished cellist and he did much to further musical interests in Toronto. He organized the Toronto Philharmonic Society in 1845 and was founder and orchestra leader of the Toronto Vocal Music Society for a number of years. Ellis also gave concerts to raise funds for charity. According to the *Commemorative Biographical Record of the County of York* of 1907, he spent his last years "at the old homestead, a picturesque spot overlooking the Humber bay and vicinity." John died in 1877, in his eighty-third year. His wife passed away seven years later.

John Ellis Jr. was a draughtsman and designer, but he retired for health reasons, devoting more time to the Herne Hill property. Shortly after his father's death, he laid out the area that later separated from York Township to become the Village of Swansea. The construction of Ellis Avenue required alteration of the waterflow out of Grenadier Pond. The remaining estate was severed and sold, and in 1930, the city purchased seventy-one acres from the Chapman family to add to High Park.

Swansea was annexed to Toronto in 1967. Ellis Avenue, Ellis Park, and Ellis Gardens perpetuate the name of the Ellises of Herne Hill.

John Ellis Jr. and his housekeeper, Mrs. Frannie Griffiths Clayton, in 1915.
The city purchased much of the Ellis estate from later owners in order to expand High Park.

RUNNYMEDE
John Scarlett

Much of the land in what later became West Toronto was reserved by the Crown for the clergy at the time of the original grants. John Scarlett was one of the first people to obtain individual title to land in the area.

Scarlett was born in Newcastle, England, in 1777, into what was presumably a prominent family of considerable means. In 1808, he arrived at York, where contemporaries described him as a handsome, intelligent, and well-connected man with several thousand pounds to his name. In York, John met Mary Thomson, a Loyalist who was also a close friend of Elizabeth Russell. John and Mary were married at St. James Church in 1810.

Mary had received the two hundred acres due to her as a loyal subject of the Crown, but John added to this about forty acres on the east side of the Humber, where he established a grist mill. The first Scarlett house, close to the river, was, according to Henry Scadding, "a large Swiss-like structure of hewn logs, with two tiers of balcony on each of its sides." This house was later destroyed by fire.

The Scarletts had four sons and a daughter between 1811 and 1826. Between 1810 and 1817, Scarlett petitioned Lieutenant-Governor Francis Gore for several pieces of land: lot 36, third concession; lot 35, second concession; lot 39, second concession; and a lease for lot 40, second concession. In all, Scarlett acquired title to four hundred acres of clergy land. He later added about 650 acres fronting on the Dundas Road, between today's Weston Road and Jane Street. Since he was the first owner of almost all of the land in the area, and the only employer for many years, John Ross Robertson declared that Scarlett "should be regarded as the father of Toronto Junction."

John was a man of strong convictions, but a gruff exterior masked a warm heart. He occupied a number of civil positions,

John Scarlett, of Runnymede, circa 1858. Scarlett acquired hundreds of acres in the Toronto Junction area. Because of this and his position as the only employer in the area for many years, John Ross Robertson dubbed him "the father of Toronto Junction." MTRL T17275

Mary Thomson Scarlett, John's wife, circa 1858. Mary was a United Empire Loyalist and a close friend of Elizabeth Russell, both of which qualified her as a member of York society. MTRL T17276

Runnymede, on Dundas Street.
From *Robertson's Landmarks of Toronto, Volume Two.*

all of which he had given up by 1821 to devote more time to his thriving businesses six miles outside York. In 1831, he opened a sawmill on the Humber. Five years later he embarked on a tour through the American Midwest with two sons to study the latest in mill machinery. Over the years, Scarlett operated brickyards, a sawmill, a grist mill, lumberyards, and a distillery, but his avocation was horses, and he was a very accomplished rider. He built a racecourse north of Dundas, west of Weston Road, in 1837, and races were held there for four years until the course closed.

As befitted a man of stature and wealth, Scarlett built a larger residence in 1838, this time on Dundas. He called his estate Runnymede. The road that ran north from his property along the Humber was already known as Scarlett's Road by that time.

In 1846, Scarlett sold his mills at Lambton to William Pearce Howland. He also began to divide his property among his sons. The arrival of the railways in the 1850s spurred initial subdivision. In 1856, Marcus Rossin bought and developed lots 39 and 40, bounded by present-day St. Clair Avenue, Jane Street, Annette Street, and Clendenan Avenue. The subdivision was called Runnymede Estate, but most of it stood vacant until 1878.

John Scarlett died at his Dundas Street home in 1865. He left Runnymede to his eldest son, Edward Christopher, who died in 1894. A number of Scarlett descendants owned land and operated businesses in the Junction. John Archibald Scarlett was a lumber and timber dealer on the Humber before he moved to British Columbia. His son bought lot 36, in the third concession, on which Gunn Abattoir established operations. Other Scarletts operated a grain dealership and a sand and gravel business in the area.

The CPR yards near Dundas and Keele spurred more development in the 1880s. Lots near Dundas sold first, while those farther away were bought by speculators. The area was incorporated as the Town of Toronto Junction in 1881, and the City of West Toronto in 1908. It was annexed to Toronto the following year. Today, two major west-end arteries — Scarlett Road and Runnymede Road — are lasting reminders of the Scarletts and their estate.

GLENSIDE
William Keele

William Keele was a lawyer in Toronto. After a brief interlude in Niagara, he moved to west Toronto in 1834 and bought a hundred acres bounded by modern Keele, Humberside, Jane, and Annette. Keele took up residence at Glenside, south of Dundas, on the concession road that was later named for him. The homestead was a roughcast mansion surrounded by a large farm. In 1840, Keele added another hundred acres, which ran south to modern Glenlake Avenue.

Keele was married twice, first to a Miss Moore, with whom he had five children, and later to Mary Clever, whose only surviving child was Charles Conway Keele.

William had the Carleton Race Course laid out on his property in 1857. The course and surrounding area appealed to Toronto families, who would venture over poor roads to enjoy a day in the country — picnicking, hunting, or ambling in the woods. The first running of the Queen's Plate was held at Carleton Race Course on June 27, 1860.

Charles Keele was educated at Upper Canada College. He later studied law, but he managed the family property rather than going into the legal profession. Charles replaced the original Glenside house with a more modern residence that faced onto Keele

Street, as it was known by then. In 1882, he sold eighty acres, including the racecourse, for $1,000 per acre, to real estate developer Daniel Clendenan. The following year, Charles married Augusta Street and they had one child, Charles Conway Jr., before Keele died prematurely in 1884 at thirty-four years of age.

Clendenan and Laws purchased the remainder of the Keele estate and laid out building lots, calling the subdivision West Toronto Junction. With the completion of the CPR Terminal at Dundas and Keele in 1884, the whole district was ripe for development, and most of the present streets were opened up as the nucleus of the Town of Toronto Junction.

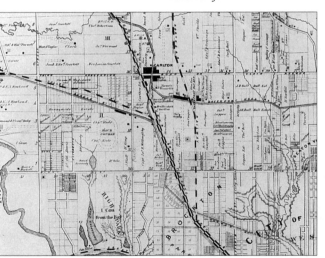

"The Map of the South West Part of York," shows Keele's estate and the Carleton Race Course laid out on his property. *The first running of the Queen's Plate was held here on June 27, 1860.* From the *Illustrated Historical Atlas of the County of York* (1878),

Although the original impetus to development in West Toronto came from the railways, the opening of the Union Stock Yards in 1903 firmly established the district as an industrial core. The Levack Company built the first abattoir, adjacent to the stockyards, in 1905. Meat packers and leather, soap, glue, and fertilizer manufacturers set up shop, becoming the major employers in the area by the time the City of West Toronto was annexed to Toronto in 1909. Only the name of Keele Street reminds us of the country estate that the Keeles once owned here, far from the bustle of the city.

For most of the 1800s, the Don River and the swampy land on its fringes were major obstacles to east Toronto's development. The government reserve, east of Parliament, was opened for subdivision after 1819, but poor drainage and the district's reputation for "bad air and pestilence" discouraged settlement. The land was not really developed until impoverished Irish immigrants escaping the potato famine moved into rental housing built on speculation in the 1840s. The tenants often grew cabbages on their meagre plots, giving birth to the name Cabbagetown. A building boom in the 1880s saw improvements in the area north of Carlton, where a mix of working-class and middle-income homes were built. East of the Don, country communities clustered around mills, but the east-end villages grew independently of Toronto because, well into the 1800s, there was only one adequate bridge across the river at Queen Street. While none of the east-end residences rival the estates west of the Don, there were several large properties that deserve attention.

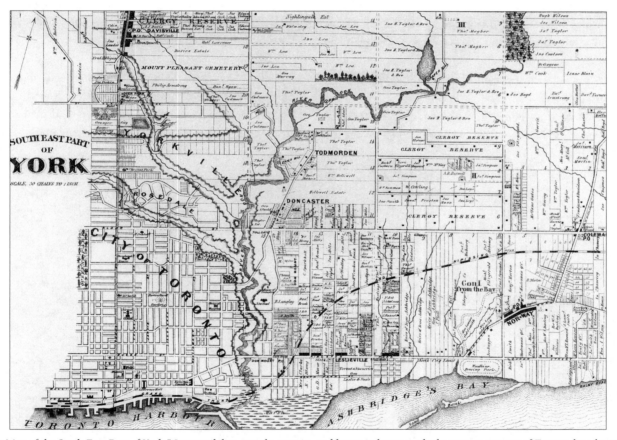

"The Map of the South East Part of York." Inaccessibility, marshy terrain, and heavy industry made the eastern sections of Toronto less desirable. Small villages, including Donmount and Leslieville, grew in isolation along the Kingston Road, quite literally the road to Kingston.
From the *Illustrated Historical Atlas of the County of York* (1878),

JOHN SCADDING ESTATE

Lot 15 ran east of the Don River to modern Broadview Avenue, and from present Bloor Street down to the lake. The 253 acres, opposite the Crown Reserve and Castle Frank, were granted to John Scadding in 1793. The landscape was rugged and hilly. White pine covered the hillsides, while a marshy delta stood at the mouth of the river. The area offered beautiful, wild views, and deer, bear, and the occasional wolf would wander through the valley.

John Scadding was manager of John Graves Simcoe's Wolford estate in Devonshire. Simcoe thought very highly of Scadding, both as a person and as an efficient property manager. A servant in the household observed that "Mr. Scadding was a very good, kind person and much liked by all classes of person." In 1792, Scadding followed Simcoe to British North America.

Scadding built his first home, a log cabin, where present-day Queen Street crosses the Don, in 1794. The only bridge to the east out of York crossed the Don there to join what was then called the Kingston Road. For many years, this crossing point was known as Scadding's Bridge, and as a familiar landmark in the area, it was used as a mustering spot for the militia.

In 1796, Simcoe returned to England in poor health. Scadding accompanied him, leaving George Playter in charge of the Don property. While back in England, in 1806, Scadding married Melicent Triggs. Simcoe gave the bride away, and the ceremony was followed by a lavish dinner at Wolford. The Scaddings had three sons: John, Charles, and Henry.

In 1818, more than ten years after Simcoe had passed away, Scadding decided to retire from Wolford and return to his own property at York. According to John Ross Robertson, he sold the original log cabin and adjoining property and used the proceeds to erect "more commodious buildings, a farm house, large barn and

Scadding's Bridge, over the Don River, and John Scadding's first house, south of Queen Street East, on the east side of the river, circa 1795.
For many years, this bridge provided the only route to the east out of York. The house was later moved to the Canadian National Exhibition. MTRL JRR T11488

Scadding's second home, north of Gerrard Street East, was built in 1818. Henry's lean-to study, at the far right, was constructed of wood salvaged from the Simcoes' Castle Frank. Much of the Scadding estate was later used for the Don Jail and Riverdale Park.
MTRL T30499

accommodation for horses and cattle." This larger home, made of carefully hewn logs, was northeast of the original, just north and west of the present Don Jail. The rest of the family came out in 1821.

On the estate, Scadding planted wheat, barley, rye, oats, and corn. His gardens included many exotic and non-native plants — Siberian crab apples, asparagus, melons, and English perennials. He improved the flats at the bottom of the valley and used them as pastures and a hop garden.

The landholdings and farming made the Scadding family fairly well off. Scadding was able to send Henry to John Strachan's school, and later to Upper Canada College, where he became the first head boy. John was also able to purchase a portion of the Castle Frank property after Francis Simcoe's death in 1812. From the rustic chateau he salvaged timber to build a lean-to on his home, for use as Henry's study. In March 1824, John Scadding was clearing brush at Castle Frank when a tree fell on him, ending his life. He was in his seventieth year.

Henry Scadding went on to attend Cambridge in 1833 on a scholarship, and later became master of classics at U.C.C. He was made the first rector of Holy Trinity Church, and, in 1867, Canon at St. James. He was a prolific writer of history, a noted religious scholar, and a founding member of several historical societies in Ontario.

John Scadding Jr. married Amelia Playter, a granddaughter of George Playter. He died in 1845, but Amelia remarried and lived on Amelia Street for many years.

The Scadding estate was subdivided during the 1850s. In 1856, Henry and his father's trustees sold about a hundred acres on the east side of the Don River to the city for £10,000, to be used for a jail and prison farm. Melicent died four years later. Riverdale Park was opened to the north of the jail in 1880.

East of the Don, isolated communities grew around toll gates along the road to Kingston. By the 1880s, these villages had grown enough to warrant incorporation or annexation; in 1884, Riverdale became part of the City of Toronto. The Prince Edward Viaduct, built during the First World War, truly opened the area to development, mostly laid out in working-class housing.

John Scadding's original cabin was preserved. The York Pioneers' Society, of which Henry Scadding was a founding member, rescued the cabin from demolition and moved it to the Canadian National Exhibition grounds in 1879. It was reassembled there and still stands as a reminder of this founding family of east Toronto.

The Playter Family home, now at 28 Playter Crescent, during the 1890s.
Playter Crescent, Playter Boulevard, Ellerbeck Street, and Jackman Avenue were all named for family members. MTRL 976-17-15

THE PLAYTER ESTATE

The two lots that ran parallel to the second concession, east of the Don, were granted to two of George Playter's sons. James Playter took lot 11, directly across the river from his father, and Eli Playter took lot 12, just north of today's Browning Avenue. Another brother, John, was granted the Summer Hill lot, but he bought his brother's Danforth property in 1831 after James had moved to Richmond Hill.

The Playters were a well-educated and upstanding family. The men occupied several public offices, while the Playter ladies maintained regular correspondence with Lady Simcoe long after her return to England. In the late 1700s, Captain George and James were assessors, Eli a town clerk, John a highway overseer, and George Jr. a deputy sheriff of the Home District. Eli later represented the North Riding of York in Parliament. Eli and George Jr. were also heroes during the American invasion of York. They took ammunition from the garrison up the Don by boat and hid it on their property. The Americans searched up the river but were finally turned back by the difficult going.

John Playter married Sarah Ellerbeck of Kingston, and they had three sons and three daughters who survived: John, Richard Ellerbeck, Emmanuel, Charlotte, Amelia (who later married John Scadding Jr.), and Sarah Anne. John gave land for St. Barnabas' Church. When he died in about 1853, he left his land to his wife. After she died, it went to their three sons. Four acres were reserved for each of the daughters.

Richard was trained in law, but poor health kept him from that profession. He inherited the property near the Danforth and immersed himself in farming. In addition to maintaining a dairy farm, orchards, and market gardens, he continued in the Playter tradition of public service as deputy reeve and magistrate. In 1845, Richard married Mary Lea. They had nine children: John Lea, Elizabeth, Richard, William, Margaret, Emma, Charlotte, Albert and Permilla. The family started selling off some property in the 1860s. The western part was subdivided and became the village of Chester. Most of the eastern lots became market gardens. Only a large parcel in the centre was reserved by the family, although the surrounding area was slow to develop because of its isolation.

Richard died in 1871. The Playter house, which stands today at 28 Playter Crescent, was built shortly after his death by one of his sons. Today's Playter Boulevard was the driveway. Richard's children continued to farm the property. John Lea Playter, born in 1846, was a market gardener and a toll collector at Broadview and Danforth during the 1870s. John married Mary Jackman in 1875. Some time later he built a large brick home on Danforth Avenue, which stood at 1 Jackman Avenue until about 1960. Emma, Charlotte, Albert, and Permilla were still unmarried and living at the farm well into the 1900s. Albert and William, also market gardeners, built a familiar Danforth landmark in 1907 — the Playter's Society Building at the southeast corner of Broadview and Danforth.

Although much of what is now Riverdale was laid out in building lots in the 1880s, development lagged. Danforth still had the feel of a country village toward the end of the century, but improving transportation was about to change all that. Between 1910 and 1915, Mary and five surviving children sold off the southern portion of the remaining estate. Playter Boulevard and Playter Crescent were opened up, and substantial homes were built before the First World War. Butternut was named for a grove of trees at the rear of the farm, and Ellerbeck for Richard Playter's mother. The end of the war and completion of the Viaduct brought development in the northern part of the former Playter estate. Browning and Fulton Avenues were opened up with affordable, working-class housing.

The Playter home remained in the family and was placed on the Toronto Historical Board's *Inventory of Heritage Properties* in 1981. Mary Lea Playter, Richard's wife, had prophesied that if the family could keep the property intact, it would someday be worth $100 per acre. In 1915, the last vacant Playter land was sold for building lots at $9,000 an acre.

THE ASHBRIDGE FAMILY

A plaque next to a rose garden on Queen Street East bears the following inscription:

> First Ashbridge Home. The Ashbridge family who came from Pennsylvania to Canada in 1793, settled here and built their home on the shores of the bay which now bears their name.

Sarah and Jonathan Ashbridge were Quakers who lived in Pennsylvania close to Philadelphia. Unlike the other Toronto estate owners mentioned here, Jonathan Ashbridge served with the colonists in the Revolutionary War. Unfortunately, before he could obtain a patent to his land, he died in 1792.

Sarah had several children to support, and she moved frequently. In 1793, fleeing plague in Philadelphia, and having heard about grants of free land, she brought her children — John, Jonathan, Elizabeth, Mary, and Sarah – to Upper Canada. They spent their first winter at York Garrison, but in the spring they set out east of the town to establish a homestead. Ashbridge family tradition has it that, along with the family Bible, Sarah brought a conch that a son blew with a great blast, marking the family's arrival in Ashbridges Bay. On the east bank of a creek, they cleared a plot and built a log cabin. Their home was surrounded by dense bush, but it proved to be fertile farmland.

In August 1796, Peter Russell granted lots 8 and 9 in the first concession, just east of modern Leslie Street, fronting on Ashbridges Bay, to the sons. Jonathan received 117 acres of lot 8, while John was granted title to 238 acres. Sarah received two hundred acres in Scarborough three years later. Notes W. T. Ashbridge in a family history, in those days,

> The necessaries of life were at times somewhat difficult to obtain. The waters were full of fine fish, and the woods with game, but to get flour, for instance, it was necessary to take the first wheat to Kingston to be ground at the mill, a distance of some 150 miles, in open boats, not a pleasant journey in stormy weather.

Jonathan's lot ran north from the lake, between modern Greenwood Avenue and Kent Road. In 1809, he married Hannah Barton. They moved into a new frame house, complete with interior walnut trim, built just in front of the older pioneer log home. One of their sons was Jesse. Another son, Joseph, died of hypothermia when he fell into the bay. The family farmed the large property for a living.

In 1854, Jesse built the first floor of the brick house that now stands at 1444 Queen Street East. A second storey and mansard roof were added in 1899. Jesse also added another fifty-six acres to the family farm. In 1864, he married Elizabeth Rooney. They they had three sons, although one died very young. The family, active Methodists, helped to found the first Methodist church east of the Don River. One son, Jesse Jr., was a brick manufacturer, and he continued to live with his mother and manage the farm after his father passed away. The other son, Wellington, worked in western Canada as an engineer, but later returned to the homestead with his family.

The family farm was kept fairly well intact until 1900, and no sizeable portions were sold until after 1905. At that time, the house still stood behind its split-rail fence, surrounded by mature elms and enjoying an unbroken view to the lake. The 1809 house was demolished just before the First World War. A portion of its foundation has been salvaged to surround the rose garden that stands there today.

A six-acre block of orchard was sold for the Duke of Connaught School, and some surrounding property was divided into small residential lots. The farm laneway became Woodfield Road. The whole district was annexed in 1909. Wellington Ashbridge inherited his father's house and farm and expanded the residence with a two-storey addition to the rear. He left the remaining estate to his two daughters, Dorothy and Betty, when he died in 1943. The house at 1444 Queen Street East was added to the city's *Inventory of Heritage Properties* in 1973, an, with its remaining two acres, is still occupied by descendants of Jonathan Ashbridge. It may well be the oldest house in Toronto continuously occupied by the same family.

The Ashbridge home, at 1444 Queen Street East, was built in 1854. On the porch is Elizabeth Rooney Ashbridge.
The 1909 Ashbridge house stood just east of this house. Some of its foundation stone now rings a rose garden on the property. Private Collection.

THREE BEACH ESTATES
John Small / Adam Wilson / Allan McLean Howard

The first of the Beach estates was John Small's farm on lots 6 and 7, immediately east of the Ashbridge properties and bounded by today's Coxwell, Danforth, and Woodbine Avenues down to the lake. Like his town home, Small named his country estate Berkeley, after his patron, the Earl of Berkeley. By 1813, Berkeley encompassed 472 acres. The youngest son, Charles Coxwell Small, took over the property in 1829 and dammed a creek to create Small's Pond, where the community of Small's Corner sprang up.

Most of Berkeley was subdivided and sold off by the late 1870s, but a grandson of the original owner, Alderman Charles Coxwell Small II, opened a section around the pond to the public in 1896. Small's Park, as it was called, was for many years a favourite pleasure spot for boating, fishing, skating, and country rambles. By 1921, construction of 150 mid-sized homes north of Small's Pond was underway, and the city approved the draining and filling of the pond for public health reasons.

Adam Wilson bought part of lots 1 and 2 in 1853 and built a summer home, just west of modern Victoria Park Avenue, overlooking the lake. Wilson was a lawyer and law partner of Robert Baldwin. He was elected Mayor in 1858 and served a second term in 1860. Three years later he was appointed to the Queen's Bench. At that time, Wilson's residence was one of only a dozen households between today's Woodbine and Victoria Park Avenues, south of Kingston Road.

During the 1870s, improvements in streetcar and steamer access made the beaches east of Toronto popular summer destinations for city residents. Resort communities and subdivision followed. In 1876, Wilson laid out his land, opening Balsam, Beech, Birch (now Silver Birch), and Pine Avenues, and setting aside a park-like promenade at the waterfront for the exclusive use of the subdivision's residents.

Wilson was knighted in 1887, and following his retirement that year, he was able to spend considerably more time at what he called his Balmy Beach Cottage. He died only four years later.

By the turn of the century, a few cottagers had put up boathouses and docks along Wilson's walkway, and residents eventually asked the city to take over and improve the stretch. The public park opened in 1904, and bowling greens, lawn tennis, and a grand clubhouse followed the next year. Adam Wilson's green space is preserved to this day as Balmy Beach Park.

In 1876, Allan McLean Howard bought thirty-seven acres on the west side of lot 2, south of Kingston Road and west of Balsam Avenue. Both Allan and his son, Allan McLean Howard Jr., were clerks for the first divisional court in the County of York. The Howard property incorporated an artificial lake, where Allan Sr. kept exotic Manchurian ducks. The treed, higher ground on the large estate was the domain of his English and Indian pheasants. Howard sold the property to his son in 1888, and the son's plan, registered in 1900, named Howard Avenue. In December 1920, the last part of the estate was subdivided into residential lots. Howard's Pond was later filled in. Howard Avenue eventually became Maclean Avenue. The Howard home still stands at the northwest corner of Queen Street and Maclean Avenue.

Adam Wilson (1814–1891) was Mayor of Toronto for two terms between 1858 and 1860. He was appointed a judge in 1863 and knighted in 1887. CTA SC 267 #92CN

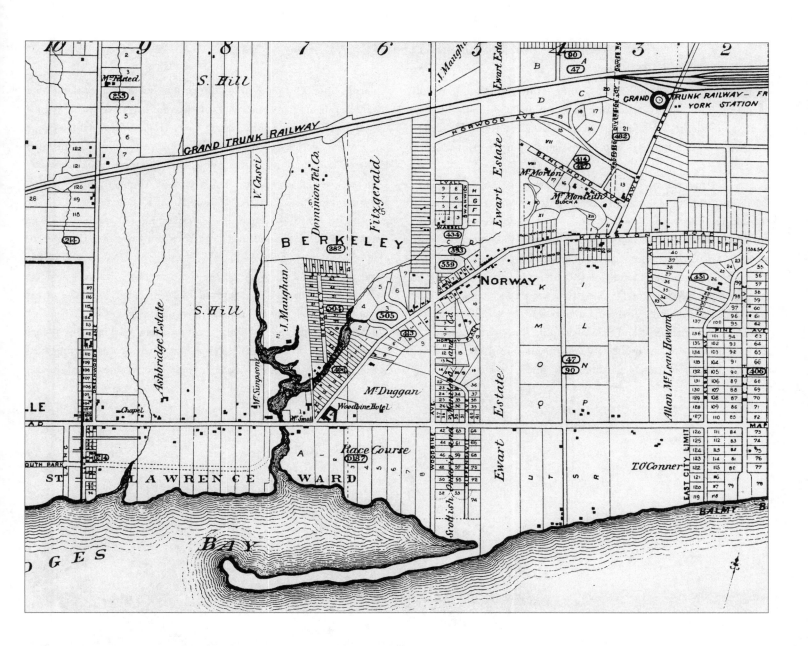

The Ashbridge estate, John Small's Berkeley, and Allan McLean Howard's property were all within Toronto city limits by this time.
Judge Wilson's estate had been subdivided to open Balsam, Beech, Birch (now Silver Birch) and Pine Avenues. From *Goad's Atlas of the City of Toronto and Vicinity* (1884).

GLEN STEWART
Alfred Ernest Ames

In 1872, Rev. William Stewart Darling, of the Church of the Holy Trinity, in Toronto, purchased property in lot 3. Soon after, he built his residence, Glen Stewart, close to Kingston Road. He died in 1886. Four years later, his son sold Glen Stewart to Alfred Ernest Ames.

A. E. Ames was born in Lambeth, Ontario, in 1866, the son of a Methodist minister. He started a highly successful career in finance at a bank when he was fifteen years old, and at twenty-three he joined a brokerage firm. In 1889, he established his own brokerage firm, A. E. Ames & Co. Ames was respected as a logical, articulate, and generous man who also possessed a kindly sense of humour. In later years, he was president and director of more than twenty large companies, including the Temiskaming and Northern Ontario Railway Commission, the Toronto Stock Exchange, and the Canada Life Assurance Company. A. E. Ames & Co. was one of the very few brokerage firms that remained solvent throughout the Depression, and Ames wrote a number of financial articles for publication, dispensing encouraging wisdoms such as, "You can vault any fence you can get your heart over."

In 1889, Ames married Mary Cox, daughter of Senator George A. Cox of Sherborne Villa. The following year, Ames bought Glen Stewart, initially as a summer home. The approach to Glen Stewart entered through large gates on Queen and wound through ravines, crossing ponds and streams, before it climbed to the house.

Ames added to the property, extending the estate from Lee Avenue to Beech Avenue, and from Kingston Road down to Queen. He made many improvements, including a trout pond, rustic landscaping, and a nine-hole golf course. He also collected an impressive library at Glen Stewart, including many volumes of his favourites — biographies and nineteenth-century novels.

In May 1905 and 1906, Governor General Earl Grey used Glen Stewart as his official residence. Ames was generous about letting local residents use his property as well; there were picnics, skating, and

This house still stands at 45 Glen Stewart Crescent, although it was greatly altered when it was divided into apartments.
From *Canadian Homes and Gardens,* September 1933.

Governor General Earl Grey used Glen Stewart as his residence during the springs of 1905 and 1906, while in Toronto for the Queen's Plate. From *The Beach in Pictures: 1793–1932.*

Alfred Ernest Ames (1866–1934), the second owner of Glen Stewart, had his own brokerage firm and was director of several prominent companies. He married a daughter of George Cox, of Sherborne Villa. MTRL JRR T30796

sleighing parties, and the golf course was opened to the public. Ames was also an active supporter of a number of public institutions and charities: Toronto Hospital for Consumptives, Gravenhurst Sanatorium, Victoria University, Beech Avenue Methodist Church, and Massey Music Hall.

In 1909, with his father-in-law, George Cox, Ames started plans for subdivision. The first plan was registered in 1910, and a development by the Provident Investment Company laid out eighty acres of the estate as Stewart Manor. In his 1923 book, *The Municipality of Toronto,* Jesse Edgar Middleton wrote:

> The tract is well wooded, and full advantage has been taken of the topography in the building of the fine crescent-shaped roads, the location, in a ravine of three artificial lakes fed from fresh water springs, and the addition of the landscape engineer's art to the prodigal gifts of nature. No pains or expense in the adaptation of this beautiful spot to home purposes have been spared by the company....

In 1931, the developers presented the ravine to the city as a park.

Alfred Ernest died at Glen Stewart in 1934. The house later underwent massive alterations and was divided into apartments. Some of the Ameses' landscaping is still recognizable, and a substantially altered coach house survives. But the more significant reminders of the Ames estate are the Glen Stewart Ravine and a number of streets — Glen Stewart Avenue, Glen Manor Drive, Glen Stewart Crescent, and Glen Ames.

CASTLEFIELD

James Hervey Price / Franklin Jackes

James Hervey Price was born in Cumberland, England, in 1797. He studied law in London and then emigrated in 1828 with his wife, Elizabeth Rubergall, her sister, and a young son. He established a law practice in York and, a few years later, purchased lot 2, in the first concession of York Township. The property ran west from Yonge Street to Bathurst, between modern Roselawn Avenue and a line just north of Briar Hill Avenue. He paid £1,000 for the two-hundred-acre parcel and very shortly afterward sold the northern half for the same amount.

Castlefield was a red-brick Neo-Gothic residence with four crenellated turrets. The main portion was two storeys high, while the two wings were one and a half. Two turrets flanked a massive double doorway that opened into a spacious central hall. The interior woodwork was of rich black walnut. The long drive (today's Castlefield Avenue) was lined with elms, and the house stood slightly east of modern Duplex Avenue. Two streams ran through the estate, and there were separate cottages for the tenant farmer and coachman, several stables, a barn, and a three-acre orchard in front of the house.

In 1834, with the incorporation of the City of Toronto, Price was appointed the first City Clerk. He was a close associate and supporter of William Lyon Mackenzie, the city's first mayor. Price provided Mackenzie and the Reformers with funds and a place for meetings, but did not support armed rebellion in 1837. It is rumoured, however, that Mackenzie hid at Castlefield after the rebel defeat. The Price's cook confronted officers at the kitchen door and railed at them not to wake the baby; Mackenzie was supposedly hidden in the cradle. Mackenzie, of course, escaped to the United States. Price was taken into custody and his offices were ransacked. He was released after thirteen days in jail.

Price sold Castlefield in 1842. Franklin Jackes purchased the estate for £1,600. The following year, Price bought lot 1 from John Montgomery and moved into the farmhouse. By 1860, Price had returned to England after dividing lot 1 into ten-acre parcels, which he sold.

The new owner, Franklin Jackes, had a bakery on King Street for many years. His most popular goods were his horse cakes — sponge cake baked in special horse-head-shaped moulds that he had made

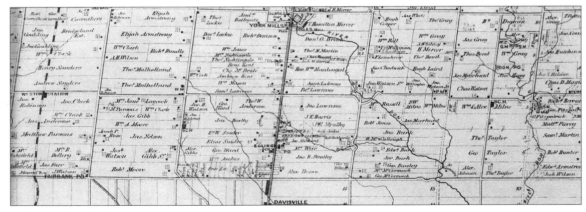

Part of "The Township of York," from the Illustrated Historical Atlas of the County of York (1878).
The Lawrence family held a number of farm properties in North Toronto. James Hervey Price's estate had already been subdivided by this time.

LEFT: *James Hervey Price's Castlefield, circa 1856. By this time, the house was occupied by the Franklin Jackes family, pictured here.* MTRL S la-736
RIGHT: *The Honourable James Hervey Price (1797–1882) was first City Clerk of Toronto, an MP for the South Riding of York, and Commissioner of Crown Lands for Canada. This portrait, by Theophile Hamel, was likely painted in 1848.* MTRL JRR T15010

himself. Jackes made his fortune during a flour shortage in 1825. Flour had to come all the way from the mills at Kingston in the 1820s, and severe storms were wreaking havoc on shipping. Jackes was waiting on the wharf one day, when a desperate agent blurted that he would sell off his long overdue shipment for £5, believing it was at the bottom of Lake Ontario. Jackes offered his savings, and, when the vessel later sailed into Toronto Harbour, he became a wealthy man.

Franklin sold the bakery to his brother and moved to Eglinton. He bought Castlefield from Price and embarked on improvements. While he was clearing and ploughing fields, he turned up pottery, pipes, and spearheads from a Native village that had once occupied the site. Later estimates placed a Huron settlement of thirty thousand people here around 1600. Jackes built display cabinets in his hallway to house the intriguing artifacts.

From 1842 to 1849, Jackes represented York Township on the Council of the Home District. In 1850, he became the first Reeve of York Township. Only two years later, he died of smallpox at Castlefield at forty-eight years of age. Jackes's eldest son, William, bought Castlefield from his mother following his father's death.

William Jackes sold the estate to developers in 1885. The Castlefield house stood for a while after subdivision, but it was demolished in 1918 to make way for Duplex Avenue. Castlewood Road, Castle Knock Road, and Castlefield Avenue all have roots in James Hervey Price's estate.

THE WILLOWS AND WILLOWBANK

James Lesslie / John Gartshore

James Hervey Price bought John Montgomery's farm lot 1, in the first concession of York Township, in 1843 and moved into the Montgomerys' farmhouse. By 1860, Price had subdivided the property into large parcels and sold them off. One of the purchasers was James Lesslie.

Lesslie bought twenty-seven acres of lot 1 in 1855 and moved into the former Montgomery farmhouse, north of Eglinton and on the east side of modern Avenue Road. He named his estate the Willows.

Lesslie was born in Dundee, Scotland. His father was a prosperous stationer and bookseller whose bookkeeper was William Lyon Mackenzie. In the 1820s, James emigrated with his friend Mackenzie and established a book and printing business, first in Kingston and then in York. In York, Lesslie, like his radical friend, was vocal about political reform, and he came to own a newspaper critical of the Family Compact. Lesslie's businesses prospered, and he later founded a bank and an insurance company. While he was busy with his commercial enterprises, he hired John Gartshore to manage the country estate and farm operations.

The *History of Toronto and County of York, Ontario*, described Lesslie's retirement to his rural retreat in Eglinton: "in his eighty-second year, he devotes his well-earned leisure to books and the management of a small farm." Lesslie passed away in 1885, leaving half of the Willows to his widow and half to Gartshore. Jacqueline received all of the household effects, and John was left the livestock and any earnings from the farm, to cover operating expenses.

Jacqueline died a few years later, and John Gartshore inherited the rest of the Lesslie estate. Gartshore built himself a larger home south of the Willows and named this new residence Willowbank. John was a strong church supporter, acting as Superintendent of Sunday School at Eglinton Presbyterian Church and sitting on the board of directors of the YMCA. He used the Willows to house visiting or retired missionaries. In the 1870s, Gartshore had also managed the Toronto Car Wheel Company, and in 1885 he founded a railway equipment business, J. J. Gartshore and Company.

James Price bought John Montgomery's house and farm lot and subdivided it. The house later became the Willows, under the ownership of James Lesslie, another vocal advocate of political reform.
Photograph courtesy Don Ritchie.

ABOVE: *John J. Gartshore's Willowbank still stands at the corner of Oriole Parkway and Burnaby Boulevard. The house was the first clubhouse for the Eglinton Hunt.* Photograph courtesy Don Ritchie.
LEFT: *John J. Gartshore. Gartshore was Lesslie's farm manager and eventual heir.*
From *Greater Toronto and the Men Who Made It.*

By the 1900s, the former Lesslie property was surrounded by subdivision. Gartshore sold the property to Lieutenant Colonel George Mitchell in 1910, and the Willows was demolished. The Eglinton branch of the Toronto Hunt Club purchased part of the Lesslie estate at that time, including Willowbank. Willowbank became the first clubhouse, and it was altered to include two new dining rooms and updated kitchens. The hunt club also built enormous brick and stone stables at the corner of present-day Elwood and Avenue Roads to accommodate up to 140 horses. An indoor polo arena was added later.

The Eglinton Hunt became independent in 1922 and later moved on to other premises outside the city. The former Gartshore estate was divided into 143 building lots. The hunt club buildings were sold to the R.C.A.F. in 1939, and a Canadian Forces Training School operated there until 1994. The Metropolitan Separate School Board owns the property now and has plans for a school and community centre.

The Gartshore house still stands at the corner of present-day Oriole Parkway and Burnaby Boulevard and is, once again, a private residence. Willowbank Boulevard runs behind it.

KINGSLAND
Samuel Huson / William Lawrence

Jonathan Hale owned the four-hundred-acre farm east of Yonge, between modern Blythwood Road and Lawrence Avenue, in the early 1800s. Hales was active in local affairs, and in his day Lawrence Avenue was known as Mr. Hale's road.

In 1836, Samuel Ames Huson paid £1,500 for lot 5, the southern portion of the Hales farm, to the intervening owner, David Graham. Huson came from a wealthy family and had property in Ireland and plantation estates in Barbados. He chose a hill on the east side of Yonge for what must have been an impressive home — Kingsland. John Howard may have been the architect. An entry in Howard's diary on April 18, 1839, notes, "Sunday at 2 Sketches of Mr. Hewsons [sic] House for him to send to the West Indies." Howard was back "to Mr. Husons to breakfast" in August of the following year, but no record of the sketches or the residence's construction survive.

Kingsland's carriage drive crossed a bridge over the ravine, near Yonge Street, and approached up a tree-lined passage that is now Lympstone Avenue. Three Huson daughters married into notable York families. In *North Toronto*, Don Ritchie wrote:

> Think back a century and a half to those weddings. Down the long drive from "Kingsland" would come at least three spotless open coaches, the horses shining, the harness gleaming and jingling. In the first coach would be the family — ladies in incredible furbelows, the gentlemen in formal coats and great stovepipe hats. In the second coach would be the bride and her attendants, excited and laughing, resplendent in new gowns…. And in the third coach would come the servants, almost members of the family for the day.

Huson died before 1845, and the family sold the estate. In 1865, William Lawrence bought the lot from intervening owners. Judging by descriptions — the Lawrence house also looked down a pine-lined drive to Yonge — the Lawrences lived in Samuel Huson's Kingsland. Henry Scadding mentioned the Lawrence home as "an English looking mansion of bricks with circular ends."

The Lawrence family had long associations with the area. In 1800, Jacob Lawrence operated a tannery at the southwest corner of Yonge and modern Lawrence. Peter Lawrence bought the farm northeast of Yonge and Lawrence in 1829 and later — at today's Glengrove and Yonge Street — built the first

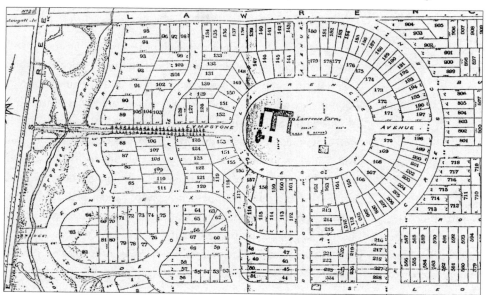

The Lawrence house, which was most likely Samuel Huson's Kingsland, stood at the top of Lympstone Avenue, looking down a tree-lined drive to Yonge Street.
From a 1910 promotional brochure for Lawrence Park Estates by the Dovercourt Land, Building and Savings Company

Dawlish Avenue, looking west, circa 1912. In the foreground is 110 Dawlish Avenue.
Behind it, to the right, is 40 St. Leonards Avenue. AO 353 Dinnick Papers

Methodist church in Toronto. Other Lawrence relations owned the lot on the northwest corner of Yonge and Lawrence.

William Lawrence married Emma Fidelia Harris, Jesse Ketchum's granddaughter. His lot was immediately north of the Harris family farm, part of which his wife inherited later. The Lawrence family farmed the property until 1907, a year after William's death.

In 1907, the Dovercourt Land, Building, and Savings Company (a subsidiary of Standard Loan Company) bought the 190-acre Lawrence farm and planned a subdivision. The mastermind behind Lawrence Park was financier and real estate developer Wilfred Servington Dinnick. He arrived in Toronto around 1870, starting out as a carpenter and eventually becoming a developer, earning, as G. Mercer Adam put it, "a handsome competence." Dinnick retained

Walter S. Brooke to lay out an upper-middle-class suburb with ravines, landscaped gardens, terraces, and curving streets. The first plan established lots of 50 by 150 feet and preserved a five-acre park in Lawrence Crescent around the old homestead. The first six homes were built by 1914, but the eastern lots were largely undeveloped until after the Second World War. With the liquidation of Standard Loan Company and its subsidiaries in 1919, many of the lots were sold at auction.

The Lawrence house and its surrounding park gave way to Mount Pleasant Road in the late 1930s, but with Lawrence Avenue, Lawrence Park, and Lawrence Crescent, the name of the second owners of Kingsland remains.

JESSE KETCHUM / JAMES HARRIS ESTATE

Jesse Ketchum was born in 1782 in New York State, but he was only five years old when his mother died, leaving behind eleven children. The father was a ne'er-do-well with a drinking problem, so the children were given up to foster homes. The eldest, Seneca Ketchum, made his way to York Township, where he bought lot 8 on the west side of Yonge Street, built a log cabin, farmed, and operated a store. Twelve years later, Jesse followed his brother to York.

The brothers shared in the hard work and profits and they were able to put aside savings. They also shared an interest in their housekeeper, Ann Love. Ann had come to the Ketchum household with a young daughter after her first husband was killed in a hunting accident. Both brothers fell in love with Ann, so they drew lots to determine who might propose. Jesse won. Fortunately, by all accounts, this coincided with Ann's wishes. Jesse, Ann, and her daughter settled on the former Jonathan Hale property, where they built a house.

The Ketchum house stood where St. Hilda's Avenue meets Strathgowan Avenue. Ketchum's biographer, E. J. Hathaway, wrote, "the original house which Jesse erected was later enlarged and rebuilt in brick, and the place, because of its picturesque setting, was known as one of the most attractive in the district." The drive was bordered on both sides by orchards. The property, between Blythwood Road and Dawlish Avenue, ran all the way to Bayview.

In 1812, Ketchum bought a tannery at the southwest corner of present Adelaide and Yonge.

The demand for boots during the war made him a wealthy man. Ketchum built an impressive town residence in York, where he could be right across from the tannery, but he held on to the pretty house at Eglinton. In 1829, Ann died, the mother of six children. Five years later, Jesse married Mary Ann Rubergall, a sister-in-law of James Hervey Price, of Castlefield, and started a second family.

The eldest son, William, set up a successful plant in Buffalo, and in 1845 Jesse moved there to manage the American business. He decided to leave the Toronto properties to his first family and to build up the Buffalo business for his second family. During the years he lived in Toronto, Jesse Ketchum was one of the city's outstanding benefactors. He provided property and funds to establish innumerable schools, churches, Sunday schools, libraries, and scholarships.

After Jesse's departure, William sold off lots on Yonge north of Blythwood and subdivided Blythwood Road. When Jesse died in Buffalo in 1867, the remainder of his Eglinton estate went to his second daughter, Fidelia, and her husband, Rev. James Harris, a Presbyterian minister. After Harris's retirement, he and Fidelia moved permanently to the Yonge Street estate, where he died in 1873. Their daughter, Emma Fidelia, married William Lawrence, who owned lot 5 to the north.

John Strathy, a financier and developer, bought eighty-five acres of the Harris estate in 1879. He named his property Strath Gowan (Gowan was his wife's maiden name). He also

Jesse Ketchum (1782–1867) grew up in a foster home and came to Canada penniless to join an older brother, Seneca Ketchum, at his farm on Yonge Street. Jesse went on to become a highly successful tanner and one of the city's most generous benefactors, helping to establish schools, churches, libraries, and scholarships.
MTRL T13792

The lane to Nicholas Garland's home, circa 1912. This was the original Jesse Ketchum house.
The drive — which today's Strathgowan Avenue follows — was flanked on both sides by orchards. AO 3718 Dinnick Papers F175-1-0-1 D119

bought twelve hundred acres around modern Erskine Avenue in 1877, which his son sold eleven years later to Nicholas Garland for double the purchase price. Garland sold the land to Dinnick's firm in 1912 at $5,000 per acre. The house was demolished in 1927.

The trees that overhung the Ketchum drive remained on what became Strathgowan Avenue. Promotional literature for the Strath Gowan subdivision recalled Ketchum's country property:

> Ere the surrounding forest had been levelled and the country entirely divided up into farms, he had chosen Strath Gowan as his homestead, building his house on the edge of the woods, fostering

and guarding with loving care the original beauties of the estate. Those to whose ownership it later passed were equally minded it should retain the glories that had endeared it to Jesse Ketchum.

Like Lawrence Park immediately to the north, Strath Gowan was slow to fill up, due to Standard Loan's bankruptcy and a glut of lots on the market. But by the late 1930s, the two subdivisions had completely transformed North Toronto from the agricultural community Ketchum had known, into a Toronto suburb of well-to-do families.

KNOCKALOE

James Metcalfe / Philip and William Ellis

Like all North Toronto estates, lot 6 on the west side of Yonge, north of present Lawrence Avenue, was granted originally as a two-hundred-acre farm lot. Four of the five lots on the west side of Yonge were granted to Joseph Kendrick and his three sons: lot 6 went to Joseph; lot 7 to Duke William; lot 8 to Hiram, who sold to Seneca Ketchum in 1806; and lot 9 to John. Joseph divided and sold his land. The Lawrence family eventually bought the southern strip, and the northern portion was later purchased by James Metcalfe.

James Metcalfe was born in Cumberland, England, in 1822, the son of a successful builder and contractor. James completed formal schooling, concentrating in math. He then entered his father's business in Manchester, where he studied architecture. In 1841, Metcalfe emigrated in search of broader opportunities in British North America. He arrived in Toronto in 1843. "Being a young man of energy, pluck and integrity, and not afraid to work, Mr. Metcalfe soon established for himself a favourable reputation," noted the *Canadian Biographical Dictionary*.

By the late 1840s, James was in partnership with two other contractors in Metcalfe, Wilson and Forbes. Their firm became very successful and won bids to build several famous Toronto landmarks, including St. Lawrence Hall, St. James' Cathedral, Trinity College, and the Toronto Normal School. Unfortunately, the partnership was unable to weather Alexander Wilson's death, and the firm was insolvent by 1852.

After the business failed, Metcalfe left for Australia, where he built several large public buildings, including the Hall of Commerce in Melbourne. He returned to Toronto in 1856 a very wealthy man and was able to retire.

In 1856, James bought part of lot 6 north of present-day Bedford Park. There he built a spacious two-and-a-half-storey brick mansion that fronted on Yonge. He had a grand, intricately carved fence imported from England to surround the lovely grounds and to confine the peacocks and other exotic birds — brought back from Australia — that wandered about the meticulous gardens. The Metcalfes spent most of their time at their town home in Yorkville, but Knockaloe, with its gardens, stables, and pastures, afforded them with country recreations befitting the family of an English gentleman farmer. Soon after moving in, Metcalfe hosted a banquet to entertain his former creditors. Under his dinner plate, each guest found the amount Metcalfe, Wilson and Forbes had owed, with interest added.

In 1886, James Metcalfe died. Three years later, two brothers, William and Philip Ellis, bought the Yonge Street estate. The Ellis brothers were prominent jewellers whose business eventually merged to become Birks-Ellis-Ryrie. Although Knockaloe had suffered extensive damage due to a fire and neglect, the Ellises restored the house and grounds and expanded the stables to accommodate their fine horses. One prize-winning thoroughbred was called Knockaloe Chief.

Development was reaching north of Lawrence by this time, and the Ellises registered a plan of subdivision, laying out Bedford Park and Woburn Avenues in 1889. They proposed fifteen hundred small lots that would form the nucleus of a factory town. Lots would sell for a very affordable $120, with a 60¢ down-payment and 60¢ instalments each week. In 1890,

Philip and William Ellis's Knockaloe.
Photograph coutesy Don Ritchie.

The Knockaloe gates at 2708 Yonge Street were imported from England by James Metcalfe.
The intricately carved fence not only provided visual interest, it also helped to confine peacocks
and other exotic birds that wandered about the Metcalfe estate. CTA James 308

the villages of Bedford Park, Davisville, and Eglinton merged to form the Town of North Toronto. One of the town council's earliest actions was to veto the Ellises' proposed factory; however, the residential development went ahead, and by 1907, the subdivision and advertising were well underway. By the time North Toronto was annexed in 1912, there were several stores and about a hundred families living on former Ellis property.

Interestingly, William Ellis opposed annexation. He led a secessionist movement from 1915 to 1920. By that time, Philip had moved farther into the city, where he was busy in private ventures and as a commissioner of several public institutions. William stayed at Knockaloe until it was sold, in 1926, to the Roman Catholic Diocese of Toronto. Two years later, the house was demolished and replaced by Blessed Sacrament School.

Many large estates were built just outside the city's boundaries during the early 1900s. Walter Massey named his 240-acre country estate and experimental farm on Dawes Road Dentonia Park, for his wife, Susan Denton. Sir Donald Mann's Fallingbrook was built, in 1907, on the Scarborough Bluffs just west of the Toronto Hunt Club. Stonedene on Bayview Avenue, Hamilton Wills' Shadowbrook at 685 Finch Avenue West, and Frederick Robins's Strathrobyn of Armour Heights are North York properties of note. The list could go on if space permitted.

Although few of the estate homes that follow are now private residences, all but Sunnybrook and Annandale are still standing and have been recognized as significant heritage buildings.

SUNNYBROOK FARMS
Joseph Kilgour

Most of the Bayview Avenue estates still stand today, and they convey the feeling of the grand country estates that existed earlier. Like the properties farther south, these estates were built just outside the city, but were still within a reasonable distance for commuting. As William Dendy and William Kilbourn put it in *Toronto Observed*:

> It is doubtful whether houses and estates on the scale of Glendon Hall, the Frank Wood house, Donningvale, and Bay View will ever be created again. For a brief period of about thirty years, from 1925 to 1955, the Bayview area was a delightful pastoral suburb on the edge of a burgeoning city.... Although the way of life they once represented has vanished, these magnificent houses and gardens — commemorating the elegance of a bygone era —fortunately remain to be seen and enjoyed.

Joseph Kilgour was one of the first to develop a country estate on Bayview. Around 1909, he bought the old two-hundred-acre Pabst farm on the east side of Bayview and named it Sunnybrook Farms. At that time, because Bayview was still a country lane and the bridge north of Eglinton flooded frequently, the approach to Sunnybrook was along what is now Sutherland Drive.

Joseph and his brother Robert established the largest packaging business of its kind in Canada, producing and printing paper bags, boxes, and wrapping paper. Joseph went on to be President of the Canada Paper Company Limited, but he was devoted to his farming and his fine horses.

Sunnybrook house was a large, rambling affair with several wings. Inside, oak panelling, an open gallery, beamed ceilings, and hunting trophies created the flavour of an English country manor. In the English tradition, Kilgour

Joseph Kilgour and his hunter, Twilight, circa 1910. Bayview was still a country lane at the time, and the district was very popular with equestrians. Kilgour's stables still stand in Sunnybrook Park. CTA James 2317

Joseph Kilgour's Sunnybrook Farms, circa 1911.
The rambling country house stood east of Bayview Avenue. The Sunnybrook
Health Science Centre stands on the property today.
CTA James 32.17

also enjoyed riding his prized hunter across the open fields and wooded hillsides. In 1913, the Kilgours hosted the first province-wide plowing match at Sunnybrook and fifteen hundred participants attended.

Alice and Joseph Kilgour had no children, so when he died, his widow donated Sunnybrook Farm to the city to be used as a park. Alice transferred the 172 acres in 1928, and entry gates on Bayview Avenue were erected in her husband's memory. The barns were preserved at the centre of what was Toronto's largest park, and its official name was Kilgour Park, although the unofficial Sunnybrook Park was eventually adopted. The Kilgour barns, which are still standing, have served over the years as a riding school, stabling for the Metropolitan Police, and as a centrepiece for field hunter trials. The Kilgour fields are now used for sports and recreation.

There was one stipulation attached to Mrs. Kilgour's gift: any use of the land for purposes other than a park would have to be approved by the Kilgours' nieces or their descendants. The Kilgour trustees

The decor at Sunnybrook Farms evoked the English country manor.
The living room opened to a gallery crowned by a beamed ceiling.
CTA James 3118

approved construction of a military hospital, which officially opened in 1946. It has since grown to become Sunnybrook Health Science Centre. The C.N.I.B. and MacMillan centres now occupy the southern part of the former Kilgour estate.

DONALDA FARMS
David Dunlap

The land flanking the Don River, just south of York Mills Road, was originally the property of a Scottish farmer named James Gray. In the early 1800s, Gray built grist and saw mills on the Don River, inspiring the name that still applies to the surrounding area — Don Mills.

In 1914, David A. Dunlap bought the Gray property. Dunlap was born on the family farm at Pembroke, Ontario, in 1863, and from a young age he was a keen outdoorsman. As he trained to become a lawyer, he spent his summer breaks prospecting in Northern Ontario. He settled in Mattawa with his mother and sister after his father's death in the late 1880s. While practising law in Mattawa, Dunlap befriended two brothers, Henry and Noah Timmins, who ran the general store.

When silver was discovered at Cobalt in 1903, the Timmins brothers and Dunlap formed the LaRose Mining Company with a few local partners. Interlopers tried to jump the claim, but Dunlap battled in court and saved LaRose's stake. The partnership went on to discover gold at Timmins in 1909 and had interests in the Hollinger and Noranda mines. Dunlap became a mining and finance magnate. When he died his estate was valued at $6 million.

Dunlap and his wife, Jesse Donalda Bell, had a Toronto residence on Highland Avenue, but they started to build a country home overlooking Gray's original millpond in 1919. Wickson and Gregg were the architects. Naming the property Donalda Farms after his wife, Dunlap expanded the estate to eight hundred acres and leased another thousand acres. The Dunlaps hoped to establish a model dairy farm, where the most innovative practices could be applied.

More than forty buildings were built or restored, and over a hundred employees saw to the needs of pampered livestock, including Guernsey cattle and Clydesdales. The cows' stalls were tiled in white, and the animals were vacuumed clean regularly. Fans kept flies down, ferns hung from the rafters, and music was piped into the barn. The Guernseys seemed to prefer Beethoven to Bach. The pigs, whose pens were lined with varnished maple, had baths twice a week. Only brass pitchforks were used, and even the pigpens had windowboxes overflowing with ivy, petunias, and geraniums.

The Norman-style frame house sits high on a hill. It is a relatively low, spreading building, but dormers and great stone chimneys add interest, as do the finely carved door trim and staircase crafted by John Ridpath. The sunroom at the front of the house, with its French doors and chintz furnishings, opened onto a tiled piazza that offered a view of the river, where swans and ducks glided beneath draping willows.

The large dining room had the ambience of an English manor, with its beamed ceiling, oak table, and great fireplace equipped with bake oven and massive andirons.

The dairy and offices of Donalda Farms occupied the ground floor of this building. Upstairs was a recreation hall, where employees and their families could enjoy music, dances, and billiards. The pigpens had windowboxes too. From *Canadian Homes and Gardens*, 1929.

Mining magnate David Dunlap started to build the house at Donalda Farms in 1919. Set high on the east side of the Don River, the residence overlooked the broad river valley south of today's York Mills Road. The Dunlap home is now the clubhouse for the Donalda Golf and Country Club.
From *Canadian Homes and Gardens*, 1929.

Here, members of the Toronto Hunt enjoyed many a hunt breakfast. Wrote Mary-Etta MacPherson in *Canadian Homes and Gardens* in 1929:

> Donalda Farm is young in actual years, but its traditions of friendly hospitality are rapidly accumulating. Looking back, I can recall few experiences with such restful country house atmosphere as I encountered here.

> Behind the house, rock gardens and manicured lawns led in terraces down to a heated swimming pool. Flowers and grass, "like broadloom," surrounded a Japanese teahouse.

The Dunlaps were active Methodists and were generous supporters of Toronto General Hospital, Victoria University, and the Toronto Art Gallery, as well as churches and educational causes.

Dunlap died at Donalda in 1924, after a two-year illness. He left the property to his wife. His hobby had been astronomy, so, in her husband's memory, Mrs. Dunlap presented funds to the University of Toronto for an observatory. The Dunlap Observatory opened in Richmond Hill in 1935.

Mrs. Dunlap continued to be active in the farm management and in numerous charities. She was elected honorary president of the Royal Agricultural Winter Fair in 1939. After her death in 1946, her son Moffatt Dunlap inherited the property. Within a few years, E. P. Taylor began planning a brewery and a housing development in the Don Mills area. Taylor's Don Mills Development Corporation bought Donalda Farms from Moffatt in 1952 and used the house as offices for some time. Eventually, they subdivided six hundred, turning the remaining two hundred acres into the Donalda Golf and Country Club, with the former Dunlap residence as clubhouse. Taylor was a moving force behind upgrading racetracks and demolishing unsatisfactory facilities. Massive wrought-iron gates salvaged from the defunct Long Branch Race Track were installed at the entrance to the club's grounds.

Although substantially enlarged, many original elements of the Dunlaps' home can still be appreciated, among them the sunroom (converted to a bar), the staircase, and, of course, the magnificent view down to the valley.

ANNANDALE UPLANDS
Herbert Bruce / Alfred Rogers

In 1920, Bayview Avenue was a favourite with equestrians, and Dr. Herbert Bruce and his wife may well have first viewed the 110-acre property they were to buy while riding on that quiet country lane. By this time, Bruce was a highly esteemed surgeon and had already established medical offices on Bloor Street and the Wellesley Hospital.

Bruce purchased the second lot south of Lawrence Avenue from the Jones family, who had farmed the property for ninety years. On the foundation of the Jones farmhouse, Bruce erected a large Jacobean mansion. He named his estate Annandale, after Robert Bruce's Scottish castle.

Eden Smith, of Wychwood Park, was the architect. The beamed ceilings, leaded-glass bookshelves, and Tudor-style fireplace all lent period flavour. The master bedroom was outfitted with its own spacious sitting room and balcony, and long windows opened from the back of the house onto the gardens.

Adele Gianelli described Annandale in *Canadian Homes and Gardens* in 1927:

> The stone lodge and garage of "Annandale" span the broad gates and driving under this medieval bridge, an avenue of cedars escorts one for a quarter of a mile, past meadowland, to the old English house whose many casement windows extend a thousand welcomes.

Stone terraces and balustrades, pergolas, and loggia complemented the formal gardens, while thickly wooded hills and pastures lay beyond. Like the house, all of the outdoor facilities were first rate, including clay tennis courts, a miniature playhouse, stabling for fourteen prized hunters, and "apartments de luxe ... provided for the pigs in a long brick building where there is everything in the way of 'parlour, bedroom and bath' for aristocratic porkers."

In 1930, Dr. and Mrs. Bruce moved to Steeles Avenue. Alfred

LEFT: *The living room at Herbert Bruce's Annandale. Architect Eden Smith included many of the Tudor details for which he was famous. Bruce used to ride from his Bayview estate through open country down to his medical offices on Bloor Street.* RIGHT: *The same room after renovations by Alfred Rogers. Rogers is reputed to have spent $250,000 on additions to the house during the depression years.* From Canadian Homes and Gardens, April 1936.

The Rogerses had elaborate landscaping done at Uplands, including this reflecting pool. Some of the landscaping survives today, although the house was torn down and replaced with a more modern home.
From Canadian Homes and Gardens, April 1936

Rogers bought the Annandale estate, substantially enlarged the house, and named the property Uplands.

Alfred Selby Rogers, the son of Elias Rogers, was born in Newmarket in 1874. Elias, who started in the lumber business, founded a coal and wood supply company in Toronto. Alfred began as a clerk in his father's company, and, after managing the head office for eight years, he purchased the firm in 1912, becoming head of one of the largest coal businesses in the Commonwealth. Later, he founded St. Marys Portland Cement Company. In 1900, he married Winifrede May Warwick. They later had a daughter, who died in infancy, and three sons.

Alfred Rogers was a prominent member of the business, sports, and social circles in Toronto. He occupied a number of corporate directorships, serving as President of Canada Building Materials, St. Marys Cement, and Elias Rogers Coal and Oil; Director of Maple Leaf Gardens, the Canadian National Exhibition, Ridley College, and Wellesley Hospital; and honorary president of the Royal Agricultural Winter Fair. Included on his long list of club memberships were the Ontario Jockey Club, the National Club, the Royal Canadian Yacht Club, the Rosedale Golf Club, and the Toronto Golf Club.

As a younger man, Rogers was an ardent cyclist, but his great passion was horses. He maintained large stables at both Uplands and the family summer home at Lake Simcoe. He won the Prince of Wales Cup in 1920 for steeplechase racing, as well as cupboards full of trophies for other equestrian events. For many years, he was Master of the Toronto Hunt and was described in papers of the day as one of Canada's greatest horsemen. Evidently, he was also a sharp dresser. In 1938, a list of the ten best-dressed men in North America, by the Merchant Tailors' Designers' Association, included F. D. Roosevelt, Jack Benny, Clark Gable, and "Alfred Rogers, Toronto, multimillionaire," much to his embarrassment.

The renovations at Uplands reputedly cost roughly $250,000 dollars during the Depression. A new southern wing incorporated a drawing room with a vaulted ceiling. Persian rugs, Chippendale and Sheraton furnishings, crystal chandeliers, and Wedgewood wall tiles lent refined opulence to the decor. The Rogers also had extensive landscaping done. A reflecting pool, lush hedges, terraces, and acres of velvet lawn surrounded the house, while the valley was equipped with riding trails.

Alfred Rogers died in 1953. His widow remained at the estate until she died two years later. Taxes and maintenance costs on Bayview had become prohibitively expensive by that time, so the family sold Uplands. The new owner, James Crothers, subsequently opened Valleyanna Drive with building lots. Uplands was replaced with a modern home, but the gatehouse, converted to a private residence, still stands on Bayview Avenue.

The Bayview Avenue gatehouse during the Rogers years.
Rogers was owner and president of Elias Rogers Coal and Wood. The gate lodge was converted into a private residence when Uplands was subdivided.
Private Collection

CLIFFORD SIFTON ESTATE

Three substantial brick buildings on Lawrence Avenue East were built by Sir Clifford Sifton in 1923 — the most impressive as his own residence, and the other two for his sons.

Clifford Sifton was born in southwestern Ontario on March 10, 1861, but moved west with his family while he was in his teens. He studied law and opened a practice in Brandon, Manitoba, in 1883. He was attracted to federal politics even at this young age, and he came to Ottawa as the Member of Parliament for Brandon in 1896, later becoming Attorney General. When Wilfrid Laurier became Prime Minister in 1896, Sifton was appointed Minister of the Interior. In that capacity, he was responsible for immigration and settlement in western Canada, and his initiatives attracted hundreds of thousands of settlers from Eastern Europe to the Canadian prairies between 1895 and 1905.

Sifton was knighted in 1915 for his remarkable contributions to Canada's development. Because of an uncompromising belief in the importance of provincial control over education, Sifton broke with

Laurier and resigned from cabinet in 1905, leaving politics entirely just six years later.

Sifton switched his attentions to business and amassed considerable wealth. In 1923, he built his home at what is now 318 Lawrence Avenue East. The impressive stone-trimmed brick house was a blend of English Tudor and Dutch design. Sifton's previous home on Sherbourne Street had been destroyed by fire, so the twenty-two-room mansion on Lawrence had poured concrete floors and steel stairs beneath its lavish finishes. The porte-cochere led to a spacious front hall with a black and white marble floor and a large fireplace. Upstairs were twelve bedrooms.

Sifton built the house at 306 Lawrence East for his son, lawyer Clifford Sifton. The most westerly house on the property was built for H. Arthur Sifton, who became Chief Executive Officer of the Sifton family's holding company. Sir Clifford, an avid horseman, also built a riding school and stables on the thirty-acre property. To the north and east of the house lay open land and the Don Valley, where he and Lady Sifton and their family enjoyed riding. The three houses, the landscaping, and the riding facilities reputedly cost over half a million dollars.

Sir Clifford died of a heart attack en route from his winter residence in Florida in 1929. In 1947, the house was sold to the Ursuline nuns. It became the Cenacle Retreat House. The younger Clifford Sifton was appointed Joint Master of the Toronto and North York Hunt, and he continued to use the riding arena, a familiar landmark just west of Bayview Avenue, until the late 1960s. The Toronto French School now occupies the house. An eastern extension was completed in 1981.

Sir Clifford and Lady Sifton in front of their home, built in 1923, at 318 Lawrence Avenue East. Sifton had retired from politics by this time, but the family had extensive newspaper and business holdings in Western Canada.
CTA James 52.24

According to the caption that accompanied this photograph in Canadian Homes and Gardens, *May 1930, The Woods' Glendon Hall achieved a "maximum of comfort and spacious hospitality. This type of house, set in the midst of its estate acres and surrounded by lawns and gardens, embodies the spirit of gracious living, and its introduction into Canadian life is very significant."*

GLENDON HALL
E. R. Wood

Edward Rogers Wood was born in Peterborough. His father was a schoolteacher, but Edward aspired to a business career. Wood was given his first job, telegraph operator at the local Canada Life Assurance office, in 1884. The company was one of many in George A. Cox's financial empire. Wood was promoted through the firm and took a posting with an affiliate, Central Canada Loan and Savings Company in Toronto. In 1901, Wood established an offshoot, Dominion Securities. Within four years, Dominion Securities was the largest bond dealer in the country and much of its success was attributed to Wood's management and direction. He had married Agnes Euphemia Smart in 1891 and had one daughter, Mildred. As a director of the Bank of Commerce, Canada Life, National Trust, the Grand Trunk Railway, and Dominion Securities, Wood became one of Canada's most affluent men.

Mr. and Mrs. Wood lived in a substantial home at Queen's Park. But in 1925, as he approached retirement, Wood purchased property at Bayview and Lawrence Avenues, retaining Molesworth, West & Secord as architects. When the Woods moved to their Bayview estate in 1925, they presented their former residence, Wymilwood, to Victoria University.

Glendon Hall occupied 125 acres — seventy in cultivated gardens and the rest in farmlands. A 1926 article in *Canadian Homes and Gardens* effused:

The gates of Glendon Hall lead to a veritable land of enchantment. Winding past an artistic lodge, the broad serpentine driveway, with its ribbon borders of shrubs and perennials intersected by groups of evergreens, gives promise of surprises ahead.

Emerald lawns, a sunken garden, rose terrace, two teahouses, trellises, pergolas, and urns spilling over with blooms adorned the formal areas. Wood also had bowling greens, turf tennis courts, and a nine-hole golf green built on the estate. From the terrace, there was a panoramic view of the valley. Rock gardens sloped down two hundred feet to the winding Don River, where the Woods had a boathouse and a diminutive, awninged pavilion on an island, for nursery teas and wading parties.

The house was a distinguished, Italian-style villa finished in stucco, with a green tile roof. The entry had a delicate ironwork porte-cochere, and urns with palmettos framed the doorway. Inside was an elliptical walnut staircase illuminated by an oval skylight. The principal rooms had ornate plaster mouldings and fireplaces faced with black and gold marble. A long gallery formed the centre of the home, with silk damask wall coverings and French doors that opened onto a loggia.

Glendon Hall, with its eminently refined decor, was also home to one of Canada's largest private collections of Dutch portraits and modern British paintings. On the second floor were bed and dressing rooms, as well as a small kitchenette for informal family refreshment.

E. R. Wood was an active fundraiser and organizer for many Toronto charities, including the YMCA, Grace Hospital, and the Orthopaedic Hospital. In business, he was noted for his astute and brilliant analysis, although in private life he was rather retiring and not particularly fond of entertaining.

E. R. Wood, the son of a Peterborough schoolteacher, started off as a telegraph operator. He founded Dominion Securities in 1901 and became one of Canada's wealthiest people. From Men of Canada

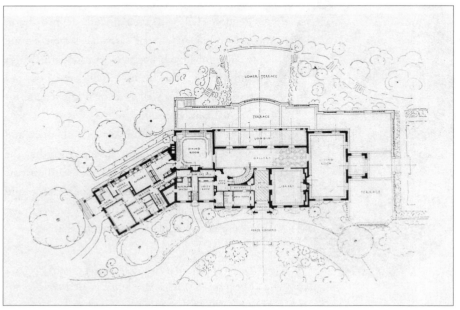

Glendon Hall was surrounded by 125 acres, much of it formally landscaped. Close to the house were two teahouses, a rose terrace, turf tennis courts, and bowling greens.
From *Canadian Homes and Gardens*, September 1926.

The first-floor plan, with its long gallery opening onto the loggia. Enormous windows could be opened to the terrace during warmer months. As part of York University's Glendon College, the terrace still offers attractive views of the Don Valley, the rose garden, and tea pavilions.
From *Canadian Homes and Gardens*, May 1930.

In 1930, Wood presented his daughter and her husband, Murray Fleming, with land on Bayview. The Tudor-inspired Chedington was purchased by Mr. and Mrs. Samuel Fingold in 1945. Most of the property was developed into exclusive condos in the 1990s.
From *Canadian Homes and Gardens*, March 1930.

The gardens and pool at Chedington.
From *Canadian Homes and Gardens*, March 1930.

In 1930, Wood gave his only daughter a portion of the estate where she and her husband, financier Murray Fleming, built their home, Chedington. The Flemings used Glendon Hall's architects, who designed a spacious home for the highest point on the property, with gorgeous views of the valley to the north and east. The house was a half-timbered Tudor building, with end gables and massive carved-oak bargeboards. Leaded casement windows, a slate roof, and a recessed front door completed the Elizabethan look.

Interestingly, when Bayview was later improved, the new thoroughfare veered three hundred metres west, so as not to separate Chedington and Glendon Hall. The slight bend in Bayview Avenue exists to this day.

E. R. Wood died in 1941. Eight years later, Euphemia presented Glendon Hall to the University of Toronto. In 1959, York University was incorporated, although it remained affiliated with the University of Toronto for its first years. The following year, the University of Toronto gave Glendon Hall to the new university, and in 1961 York University moved onto its own Glendon campus. Since the opening of the main campus in Downsview, the former Wood property has become York's Glendon College. Chedington was purchased by Samuel Fingold in 1945. The house is still a private residence, although exclusive condominiums now occupy most of the property. The house received heritage designation in 1994.

FRANK P. WOOD ESTATE

Frank Porter Wood, a younger brother of E. R. Wood, was born in Peterborough in 1882. Frank left Peterborough as a teenager and took a job as a clerk in Montreal. A lifelong interest in art was evident even in those early years; Frank spent most of his first month's pay on a painting.

Frank pursued a career in finance and was every bit as successful in that field as his older brother. He moved to Toronto and later became a founding member of the brokerage of Baillie, Wood and Croft, President and Chairman of Burlington Steel, Vice-President of National Trust, and a director on the boards of several financial institutions. Both Frank and E. R. Wood were principals in the formation of the Brazilian Traction Company, which later became Brascan.

In 1928, Wood purchased just over thirty acres from the Bayview Heights Limited development corporation. The property, with grand views of the Don Valley to the west and south, cost $90,000 and was just across the Don River from Glendon Hall. The contract for construction was awarded in the summer of 1930, with a projected cost of $400,000. The bridge over the Don was just being upgraded in 1930, improving access to this stretch of Bayview Avenue.

Wood used the architectural firm of Delano and Aldrich, a New York firm well known for designing prestigious Astor and Rockefeller homes, among others. The architects' plans are today held in the Columbia University archives in New York.

Delano and Aldrich trained at the eminent Ecole des Beaux-Arts in Paris. As a result, the Wood home has the air of a French country house, with a few added American Colonial elements. Made of smooth-cut limestone, the house design was symmetrical and elegant.

Louvred shutters, a high slate roof, and an octagonal window above the entry contributed to the French look. An interesting hexagonal cupola shed light on the main stair. The forecourt was paved in brick and stone and fronted by low, curving walls, while the stables formed the north wall. On the south end of the house, a five-sided Regency-style sunroom looked out on paved terraces through great windows supported by slender bronze verticals.

The garden design was formal. Full-length French windows on the main floor offered a view of a long manicured lawn hedged neatly by shrubs and culminating in a picturesque columned structure at the south end. A fountain, a sundial, climbing roses, and ivy contributed to the French country ambience.

Wood's passion was collecting fine art. With his family, he toured galleries in Europe and expanded his impressive private collection. His wife and children always had to approve his selections; a Van Gogh was returned following their veto. Wood's most famous acquisition was a portrait by Dutch master Frans Hals, which reportedly cost $195,000. Wood was also a great benefactor of the Toronto Art Gallery (now the Art Gallery of Ontario). He donated works by Gainsborough, van Dyck, and Rodin during his lifetime and bequeathed the rest of his collection and his home after his death.

Frank Wood died in 1955. The Bayview Heights house was sold to George Weston, and the proceeds went into a foundation used to purchase paintings for the gallery. The Frank P. Wood Gallery at the AGO was named to recognize his significant contribution. In 1967, The Crescent School, a private boys' school, purchased the property. The house still stands at the centre of the school complex.

Frank Wood was a younger brother of E. R. Wood of Glendon Hall. Frank's home was designed by a New York firm, Delano & Aldrich,
known for their architectural work for the Astors and Rockefellers. The cupola shed light on the impressive staircase. Photograph by Liz Lundell.

BAYVIEW
James Stanley McLean

J. S. McLean was born in Durham County in 1876, the son of Colonel William and Sarah McLean. He received his B.A. from the University of Toronto in 1896 and then tried his hand at teaching for two years. In 1901, he took a position as a clerk at the Harris Abattoir Company and embarked on a highly successful business career.

In 1927, Harris Abattoir, having acquired Gunns Limited and the Canadian Packing Company of Canada, merged with William Davies Limited under the holding company of Canada Packers Limited. The chief architect of the amalgamation was McLean, and he was elected president of the new meat processing giant, a position that he held until retirement in 1954.

In 1912, James married Edith Flavelle, a niece of Sir Joseph Flavelle, who was a partner in William Davies. They later had one son and two daughters. In 1928, they bought just under fifty acres on the east side of Bayview Avenue and commissioned architect Eric Arthur to design a country mansion. The McLeans took up residence in 1931.

Arthur's design was reminiscent of eighteenth-century English estates. The Georgian-style house had a steep slate roof with dormers, and its fieldstone walls were graced with large and harmoniously proportioned windows. The main entry, flanked by Corinthian columns, entered from a gravelled forecourt on the east side of the house. Just inside, a high arched window illuminated an elegant spiral staircase. Across the main hall, a comfortable library and bright drawing room occupied the garden front of the residence. The mahogany-and-walnut-panelled dining room occupied the north wing, while the south wing held a sunroom that opened out onto a terrace, with views of the carefully designed gardens and the expansive Don River Valley.

Landscape architect Gordon Culham planned magnificent gardens that completed the grand impression. Culham used spreading lawns and carefully placed trees, shrubs, and ornamental beds to achieve a quintessentially English look. The formally arranged garden

at the front of the house offered a long vista, through a parterre with a fountain and across a turf badminton court, to the rose garden. A feature in *Canadian Homes and Gardens*, in 1934, described the pleasing effect:

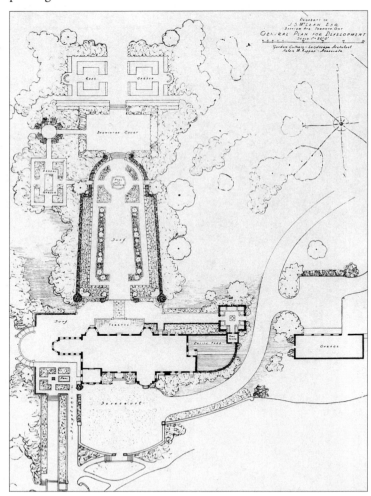

The garden plan by landscape architect Gordon Culham. The sunroom at the left side of this plan has a stunning view east toward the Don Valley.

J. S. McLean's Bayview looks much the same today from the outside. Now a catering and conference centre,
all proceeds from McLean House, as it is now called, go to Sunnybrook Health Science Centre. From *Canadian Homes and Gardens*, September 1934.

The driveway curves through thick woods and between banks planted with clumps of Azaleas … to emerge finally into an open sunlit park where there is a seemingly endless expanse of emerald lawns, studded with fine trees. The house, charming and dignified in the early Georgian manner, crowns a slight eminence.

J. S. McLean died in 1954, and his son, William F. McLean, succeeded him as President of Canada Packers. The family remained at Bayview until Mrs. McLean died in 1967. Prior to her death, the University of Toronto expropriated Bayview to provide land for expansion of Sunnybrook Health Science Centre. The residence temporarily housed the Donwoods Institute and was later used as office space for the hospital.

In 1983, the Junior League and Interior Designers of Ontario refurbished Bayview as part of a fundraising showcase. The house became a conference centre and a special-events facility. Today, the McLean estate plays host to business gatherings and social functions, from garden weddings to black-tie fundraisers, and the proceeds go toward medical research.

DONNINGVALE
John James Vaughan

John James Vaughan was born in Toronto in 1881. His father was Robert Vaughan, who retired from an early career with the police force to start up a contracting business. John was one of five sons. One of the brothers, Joseph, went into the contracting business and later developed the Summerhill estate. John, on the other hand, had a flair for finance. After graduation, he took a job with a railway and studied business and finance in his spare time.

In 1903, J. J. Vaughan joined the T. Eaton Company as a junior clerk. He worked his way through the ranks and earned a reputation for keen intelligence and attention to detail. In 1907, he was appointed Secretary of the company, and in 1917 he was made a director. Vaughan was both a trusted business advisor and close friend of John Craig Eaton. He had a head for figures and, in the words of his contemporaries, was able to use numbers "like weapons" to accurately assess a situation and support sound business decisions. After John Craig's unexpected death in 1922, E. Y. Eaton took over the company presidency. He was able to rely heavily on Vaughan as Director and Secretary-Treasurer to get the company through that difficult period. Vaughan was promoted to Vice President in 1933.

Vaughan married Estelle Leslie, and they had two sons and a daughter. When Herbert Bruce sold Annandale, Vaughan bought the southern portion of the property and had Burden & Gouinlock design a new residence. In 1931, the Vaughans moved from their former home on Glen Road to their impressive country estate.

The drive entered, as it does today, through stone gateposts inscribed with the estate's name — Donningvale. The grey-stone residence stood in the centre of a private park. Two gabled wings at either end flanked a gabled main entrance. The straightforward design had an Elizabethan simplicity complemented by thoughtfully placed plantings designed by landscape architect Gordon Culham. In an article in the *Toronto Star* in 1982, Donald Jones described the approach to the house "at the end of a long and winding driveway that passed a broken forest and acres of manicured lawn and flower beds. Finally rising on the crest of a hill, the house bursts into view, its walls and gables covered in dense ivy and looking like some vast baronial manor house." On the east side of the house, a loggia opened out from the hall taking in the views of the thickly forested Don Valley.

J. J. Vaughan was a founding member of the Toronto Art Gallery and of Maple Leaf Gardens. The Vaughans were active supporters of many of Toronto's charitable institutions. It is thus fitting that the house stands today as part of a teaching hospital and medical research facility.

In 1966, three years after Vaughan's death, Donningvale was expropriated as part of the plan to expand Sunnybrook Medical Centre. The grand house was boarded up and was neglected for many years. During the 1970s, the building was used for a substance-abuse rehabilitation program, but after that organization's departure, the residence was abandoned once again.

In 1989, encouraged by the success of the McLean estate, organizers proposed refurbishing the Vaughan house to create another facility for business and social functions. Extensive restoration followed. The Vaughan Estate, as it was renamed, opened as a conference and catering centre in October 1991. It is now rented out for business and private functions. All profits are directed to research at Sunnybrook Health Science Centre.

Donningvale, better known today as the Vaughan Estate, was built by John James Vaughan, Director and Vice-President of the T. Eaton Company.
Photograph by Donald Standfield.

PENRYN
Norman D. Perry

Colonel Norman Perry, circa 1928. Perry rode with the Glen Mawr Riding Club, whose base was in the Don valley, just north of Glendon Hall. Perry committed suicide by jumping off a bridge, but it was kept out of the papers. CTA James 1352

This impressive residence at 9 Versailles Court was surrounded by orchards and fields when it was built in 1932. Penryn was originally the home of Colonel and Mrs. Norman D. Perry. Perry was president of Assurance Securities Corporation. He was also an avid horseman. The Perrys had Toronto architects Mathers and Haldenby design their home, as did several other prestigious residents in the area during the 1920s.

Much of Penryn's elegance comes from its formal Georgian Revival design. Built of red brick, with stone detailing, the stately, symmetrical home had nineteen shuttered windows and three dormers on its north face. Inside, a central hall, fine wood trim, and dignified furnishings reflected the Georgian influence. Chinese porcelain lamps and fine fabrics ensured an airy and sophisticated look. A portrait of Mrs. Perry by Kenneth Forbes hung prominently in the dining room.

The Penryn property was used as an orchard before the Perrys built their home. Many of the apple trees were preserved during landscaping. Low stone walls surrounded a sunken area with a formal rose garden. Beyond lay a manicured lawn flanked its entire six-hundred-foot length by lush perennial borders. An enchanting white teahouse stood at the far side of the lawn. In the Perrys' time, the house was approached by way of what is now York Mills Road, past rolling countryside, and then up an elm-lined drive. Colonel Perry took advantage of this rural setting, joining the Glen Mawr Riding Club, whose facilities were in the Don Valley, just north of Glendon Hall.

Penryn was featured in *Canadian Homes and Gardens* in 1934 and 1938, but mention of Colonel Perry's death is notably absent from newspapers and journals, and the date of his widow's departure from Penryn is unpublished. The property was subdivided much later when Versailles Court was opened up in 1970. Several of the homes built on that street in the early 1970s take their stylistic direction from Penryn, now a historically designated house.

Penryn, the home of Colonel and Mrs. Norman D. Perry, was built south of York Mills Road, east of Bayview, in 1932. It stands at the head of modern Versailles Court in North York. From *Canadian Homes and Gardens, 1934.*

Bayview and Lawrence Avenues from the southwest, circa 1930. The Siftons' large riding arena occupies the bottom left, and the two Sifton houses in front of it are now the Toronto French School. On the east side of Bayview stands Chedington. Glendon Hall and its circular forecourt are slightly right of centre. Uplands and its large lawns are next on the right, and Donningvale stands at the end of its long drive on the right edge of the picture. E.P Taylor was to build Windfields on Bayview (just beyond left edge) in 1936. Today's Bridle Path runs parallel to the top edge of the photograph. CTA James 2433

WINDFIELDS
E. P. Taylor

Edward Plunkett Taylor was born in Ottawa on January 29, 1901. It was probably from his maternal grandfather, businessman and brewery-owner Charles Magee, that Edward acquired his early interest in business.

Taylor was a resourceful and energetic youth. During a summer's apprenticeship in a machine shop, he invented a toaster that could brown both sides of the bread at the same time. Selling the rights earned him his first big money — several thousand dollars. E. P. graduated from McGill University with an engineering degree in 1922 and joined McLeod, Young, Weir as a bond salesman shortly after. In 1927, the year Prohibition was repealed, Taylor married Winifred Duguid. Two years later he was promoted to junior partner and moved to the head office in Toronto.

The end of Prohibition brought opportunities. Taylor had studied the Ontario brewing industry closely, and in 1930 he incorporated the Brewing Company of Ontario. Under Taylor's management, small, inefficient breweries were bought up and merged into a larger, more profitable operation, eventually known as Canadian Breweries. Taylor was responsible for increasing stock prices from 25¢ to $24 a share between 1931 and 1949.

The Taylors rented the Sifton house on Lawrence Avenue East late in 1930. They bought their own Bayview property two years later, but were unable to build until 1936. That was also the year that E. P. bought his first racehorse, launching him on a course that would earn him more lasting renown than all of his business endeavours.

The Taylors moved into the new home with their two daughters and one son in 1937. The two-storey stone house had a long, low design, and it was surrounded by flower gardens, hedges, and hundreds of acres of open fields. The American Colonial design included a simple facade, a Palladian window above the front entry, a low slate roof, and an elaborately carved doorframe topped by a pineapple pediment — the colonial symbol of hospitality.

Inside, the south wing housed staff bedrooms, a kitchen, and a staff lounge. The central dining room enjoyed an expansive view of the gardens east of the house. Taylor's panelled study next door was comfortable but unpretentious. The formal living room, or "garden room" as the Taylors referred to it, stretched across the north end of the house, and French doors opened onto a terrace and the garden. Above the main staircase, illuminated by the Palladian window, stood a sculpted plaster frieze of racing horses. The stair balusters were decorated with metal ribbons tied in whimsical bows. The Taylors built a private movie theatre in the basement and a stable for four horses right next to the house. Eventually, they added tennis courts and a swimming pool.

There were few mature trees on the property. Taylor promised $100 to any of his friends able to come up with an appropriate name for the estate. None appealed to him, until Winnie, inspired by the wind gusting across the fields one fall day, suggested "Windfields." Apparently, she never received her prize money.

During the war, E. P. served as Director General of Munitions and Supply and was one of C. D. Howe's "dollar-a-year" men in Ottawa. With Howe, he survived nine hours in a lifeboat after their ship was torpedoed in the North Atlantic.

After the war, Taylor added to the house and built gatehouse offices. His corporate headquarters were still in Toronto, but the Windfields cottage provided office space for seven personal assistants, who supported Taylor's energetic schedule.

In 1945, with Eric Phillips, Bud McDougald, and Wally McCutcheon, Taylor formed the Argus Corporation. Like so many other Taylor enterprises, it was the first corporation of its type in Canada. Argus invested in companies where it could gain controlling interest with a relatively small proportion of total shares, and its holdings included Massey-Ferguson, Dominion Stores, Standard Broadcasting, and Domtar. In 1968, sales from Argus-controlled

This photograph of E. P Taylor, taken at Windfields in 1941, was published in the Globe *and* Mail.
During the war, Taylor served for a salary of one dollar per year in munitions and supply. CTA SC266.71562

companies represented a higher percentage of this country's gross national product than General Motors did in the United States. The spreading tentacles of Argus alarmed many and earned Taylor the sobriquet "Excess Profits" Taylor.

Taylor was involved in the housing development on the west side of Bayview, south of York Mills, planning large lots and one of Canada's first shopping plazas. He also masterminded the planned community of Don Mills. The initial idea was to build a brewery and then construct housing for its employees in the vicinity. Taylor had to give up the brewery plan, but between 1952 and 1960 he was able to develop land purchased through the O'Keefe Realty Company. Don Mills won awards for balanced land use and new approaches to row housing. Interestingly, Taylor disliked blue roofs because they faded and were unattractive in bright sun, so there were no blue shingles in

Don Mills. About this time, Taylor sold half of his eighteen-hole golf course to IBM and let his herd of Angus cattle graze on the remainder.

Taylor was also a quiet philanthropist; most of his donations were made anonymously. But it was Taylor who established the foundation to build the O'Keefe Centre (now the Hummingbird Centre) in Toronto.

Over time, Taylor added to his Bayview property to the north and east, and Windfields Farms became famous as a thoroughbred breeding and training facility. Taylor's property eventually included a thousand acres stretching from Bayview to Leslie Street, and from points as far south as Post Road north to Highway 401. North of York Mills Road were a half-mile track, paddocks, training barns, and housing for stable staff. South of York Mills was the breeding operation, with separate barns for stallions, mares, and mares with foals. In 1964, Northern Dancer brought fame to Windfields when he won the Kentucky Derby and Preakness, and members of the royal family often stayed at Windfields when in Canada for the Queen's Plate.

By 1971, Taylor had rejuvenated racetracks and betting in Canada and had bred 10 Horses of the Year, 14 Queen's Plate winners, and 112 stakes winners. He had also established the National Stud Farm, in Oshawa, on former McLaughlin property.

The late sixties brought many changes. Taylor sold Windfields to eager developers for $12 million and bought a breeding farm in Maryland. The family reserved thirty acres for parkland in the City of North York and left the house and surrounding twenty acres to the city as well. By this time, the Taylors had already moved their principal residence to the Bahamas, where Taylor developed an exclusive enclave — Lyford Cay. He became a citizen of the Bahamas in 1977.

Taylor suffered a stroke in 1980, and Winifred died two years later. In 1986, Norman Jewison leased Windfields for a centre for a new film academy. Windfields reopened after alterations in February 1988, and today the Canadian Film Centre offers advanced training to writers, directors, producers, and editors in both television and film.

E. P. Taylor died in Lyford Cay on May 14, 1989. Peter Newman wrote at that time, "Taylor is an important figure in Canadian business history because he was the last and most successful of his breed...." Some saw him as a robber baron, others as a shrewd visionary, but no one disputes the enormous contribution of E. P. Taylor and Windfields Farm to thoroughbred breeding and racing in Canada.

GRAYDON HALL
Henry Rupert Bain

Henry Rupert Bain was born in Prince Albert, Saskatchewan, in 1898, but he moved to Toronto after his father died in 1903. He later attended Harbord Collegiate. He served with the Canadian Expeditionary Force during the First World War and joined a brokerage firm after his return in 1919. In 1923, at twenty-five years of age, Bain set up his own brokerage in Toronto — H. R. Bain and Company.

The firm initially dealt in municipal and corporate bonds, but Bain switched to mining finance in 1934 and became the first broker to promote gold stocks during the Depression. It was Bain who financed the Pickle Crow mine. His panache, bold schemes, and knack for advertising paid off, as he became a self-made millionaire. Bain was later Vice-President of the Fanny Farmer Candy Shops and President of the National Life Assurance Company.

Bain purchased property on the east side of the Don River, north of what is now York Mills Road, in 1934. The property was originally farmland, but Bain transformed the hundred acres. The name — Graydon Hall — may have been inspired by the first local mills on the Don River, built by James Gray.

Bain retained architects George and Moorhouse, and the house was completed in 1936. A twenty-nine-room Georgian manor, Graydon Hall was constructed of fieldstone, with fine Indiana limestone trim, at a total cost of $250,000. It had fourteen bedrooms and a ten-car garage, and its grandeur was topped only by Casa Loma.

The entry faces a forecourt paved in brick and stone, and a porte-cochere supports an upper balcony surrounded by a stone parapet. A large Palladian window lights the stair hall, while above the door, a broken pediment is adorned with a carved floral swag and an urn. "A.D. 1936" is prominently chiselled into a stone plaque. The main-floor windows are very tall, and the roof is steeply hipped and tiled in blue-grey slate. Elegant stone ornaments abound.

The interior boasted Chinese hand-painted wallpaper, antique Persian rugs, and ornate mouldings and panelling. Apricot taffeta drapes graced the breakfast room. The drawing room had deep bay windows, walnut panelling, and an eighteenth-century gilt mirror. At the west end of the house was the sunroom.

The garden was cleverly hidden from the approach by artificial hills and walls. The only way to gain access was through the house, where the breathtaking views were shown to greatest advantage. As they stepped through double doors on the garden facade, visitors found themselves on a balustraded stone terrace. The gardens, designed by Dunnington, Grubb, and Stensson, were laid out in distinct formal courts across the back of the house. The flower garden was flanked by a path that ran beneath arches covered with climbers, and a tea pavilion and lawn promenade led to a formal fountain court. From the fountain, water bubbled down to an informal pool and then on to limestone pools and cascades that fell, in series, between rock gardens and down to the woods.

A self-made millionaire, H. R. Bain enjoyed a lavish lifestyle. He bred horses and was a competitive polo player.
Bain, on the left, receives a trophy from Jack Hammell in 1926. CTA James 2335

The dining room at Graydon Hall. The portrait shows Aileen Bain, Rupert's first wife, who married his close friend in 1951. Bain subsequently married his friend's former wife. From *Canadian Homes and Gardens*, 1938.

The Bains also had a nine-hole golf course and stables, where Rupert kept his polo mounts and the hunters he rode as Master of the Fox Hounds of the Eglinton Hunt. He raised Great Danes, mastiffs, and Newfoundlands on the property, and bred racing horses. The Hunt club's hounds were kept at kennels on Graydon Hall property from the late 1930s until 1950, when Bain sold that parcel to E. P. Taylor for development.

In 1951, Bain's friend Reginald Watkins divorced his wife and married Mrs. Bain. One week later, Bain married the former Mrs. Watkins. Shortly afterward, Bain sold Graydon Hall to Nelson M. Davis, president of Intercity Forwarders and head of a transportation and construction empire of about fifty companies. Interestingly, the N. M. Davis Corporation had its offices at Penryn for some time.

Rupert and his new wife spent much of their time travelling, often to Bermuda. He died on March 25, 1952, at fifty-four years of age, while vacationing in Mexico. He left behind legal wrangling over who should be considered his rightful widow and beneficiary of an estate worth $1,234,000. The courts eventually decided in the first wife's favour.

Nelson Davis sold Graydon Hall to Normco Limited and Combo Construction in 1964 for well over one million dollars. Today, the house is in the middle of a subdivision overshadowed by high-rise apartment buildings, although part of the property remains intact. The current address is 185 Graydon Hall Drive, and a convenience store, hairdresser, and recreation facility occupy the east wing of the house. The main part of the residence is vacant and neglected, although it was recently designated as a heritage structure. Tucked away, Graydon Hall is still both graceful and imposing in spite of overgrown gardens and vandalism to the terraces.

The garden front of Colonel Eric Phillips' Wynyates. The house was built during the Second World War, before Phillips helped to found the Argus Corporation. At the eastern end of the colonial style home, a terrace adorned with fretwork supports a second-floor balcony. Photograph by Liz Lundell.

WYNYATES
W. Eric Phillips

Built during the Second World War, Wynyates, with its Colonial Revival style, is far less grand than the pre-war estate homes. The two-storey, white, painted-brick building still stands at 10 Buchan Court, northeast of Sheppard Avenue and Leslie Street, behind the Bloorview MacMillan Centre.

The house was completed in 1945 for Colonel W. Eric Phillips. Born in Toronto in 1893, Phillips graduated with a degree in Science from the University of Toronto in 1913. He served with British regiments during the First World War until he was wounded in 1918, and he resigned his commission in 1920 after receiving the Distinguished Service Order. In 1918, Phillips married Mary Eileen McLaughlin, whose father was R. S. McLaughlin, president of General Motors, but they divorced about twenty years later, before Wynyates was built.

Colonel Phillips established a glass company in 1922, which manufactured safety glass for the automotive industry as well as other products. During the war, Phillips assisted the Canadian effort as president of Research Enterprises. It was there he that he met E. P. Taylor, who was greatly involved in war industry and supply. About that time, Phillips sold part of the company to Pittsburgh Glass. He suddenly found himself with a great deal of money. He remarried in 1940 to Doris Delano Gibson and started construction on his country estate just four years later.

After the war, Phillips joined Taylor, lawyer Wally McCutcheon, and businessman Bud McDougald in forming the Argus Corporation. Argus was named for the son of Phrixus in Greek mythology, who built the ship used on the voyage to discover the Golden Fleece. Argus Corporation was the first close-ended investment fund of its kind in the country. Wide diversification and controlling interests acquired with small percentages of stock were its hallmarks. Its influence was so widely felt that on June 5, 1964, ten percent of the trades on the Toronto Stock Exchange were in Argus-controlled companies.

Phillips was a director of more than a dozen companies. He was closely involved with the restructuring of Massey-Ferguson and with restoration of the Bank of Toronto building at 10 Toronto Street. He also served on the Board of Governors at the University of Toronto and on the Board of Trustees for Toronto General Hospital.

The country home at Wynyates was ready in 1945. The three-bay pedimented central portion lends a definite colonial flavour, but instead of the symmetry one might expect, the layout is rather irregular. The two-bay wing on the east has a ground-floor verandah adorned with delicate woodwork and an upper deck. The wing to the west has one pair of windows on the front and a lower two-storey section jutting out towards the driveway. Smaller additions were made to the north and west of this section. The entry is understated compared to the doorways of the other estate homes. A rectangular transom is decorated with lacy Adamesque tracery.

The entry leads to a large reception room that opened out onto the south terrace and gardens. The dining room has deep wall niches, impressive ceiling mouldings, a fireplace with a carved mantel, and a view to the south gardens, where an orchard once stood, but the interior has been greatly altered to accommodate offices. Detractors criticize the building for its jumble of styles and lack of presence, but its black shutters and crisp white paint give the large house a smart, solid appearance.

Phillips died in 1964; his wife died in 1980. The house is surrounded now by subdivisions and medical facilities, and it is owned and leased by the North York General Hospital. Wynyates has been home over the years to a number of agencies, including the Renascent Treatment Centre and the Metropolitan Toronto Association for the Mentally Retarded. Colonel Phillips's home was added to the City of North York's Inventory of Heritage Properties as one of several country estates built during the first half of the 1900s by members of Toronto's business elite.

EPILOGUE

One must always maintain one's connection to the past and yet ceaselessly pull away from it.
To remain in touch with the past requires a love of memory.
To remain in touch with the past requires a constant imaginative effort.

GASTON BACHELARD (1884–1962)

Looking at Toronto's old estates is a bit like returning to a room the morning after a large reception. Amid the clutter, a few mementoes remain. The odd bit of greenery droops where formal arrangements flourished. A forgotten scrap of paper hints at what occurred. With luck, someone took a photograph. But the dazzling moment has passed, mostly unrecorded and never to be recaptured entirely accurately.

The stories of these estates survive in much the same fashion: a few printed words, the odd photograph, some architectural artifacts, and memories. Several estates, especially the earlier ones, were not thoroughly chronicled. People didn't — and perhaps still don't — keep records and photographs of their own homes. Nor did estates fit handily into established subject areas in the days before "local history." A description of the house or the life of the patriarch who built it does not provide a complete picture of the estate. That must touch on several disciplines, including biography, architecture, history, and urban studies.

Even at that, our image of life on these large properties remains incomplete. The estates existed as a result of the efforts of a great number of unmentioned people: the builders, household staff, tenant farmers, gardeners, and workers who the property owners employed. That privileged lifestyle was costly in terms of the labour required to support it. Small wonder that the estates rarely remained intact as they passed to the third generation or were sold out of the family.

These estates belong to Toronto's past, but they also explain quite a bit about the city's present arrangement. Most major north–south streets below Bloor ran the length of an individual property. East–west roads were opened as short streets across the width of a property and were not necessarily planned to join up with those on neighbouring estates. Our neighbourhood boundaries, and often their character, owe much to early subdivision plans. Some districts still bear the name of the original estate, including Rosedale, Dovercourt, Playter Estates, Deer Park, Rathnelly, and Summerhill.

The most observable relics of the great estates are most certainly street names. T. A. Reed observed in 1929:

> It has often been truly said that the history of a city can be read in the names of its streets. They are monuments that often tell more and speak more eloquently than statues of marble or bronze…. Here in Toronto we are rich in street names that mean something, names that should be treasured as so many pages in our city's history.

A Toronto map reads like a history of the city, and a walk down Woodlawn, Roncesvalles, Spadina and many others reminds us of the estates and of the people who subdivided and provided names for these streets.

Our "love of memory" and "imaginative effort" are perhaps best indulged, though, with a visit to the homes that have been carefully preserved and are now open to the public. The servants' domain is recreated in the basement kitchen at the Grange, while the upstairs has been restored to the grandeur of an 1830s gentleman's home. Approaching Colborne Lodge, the distinct feeling of leaving the city behind to reach the country estate remains intact. Tea and cakes are laid out on fine china in Spadina's parlour. Casa Loma's Great Hall, Donningvale's sweeping drive, and the gardens at Bayview or Glendon Hall make the connection with the past palpable. In the presence of these great homes, it is easy to cast our thoughts back and imagine life on the expansive estates that were subdivided to create modern Toronto.

BIBLIOGRAPHY

"Annendale House: Estate of Dr. Herbert Bruce." *Canadian Homes and Gardens*, February 1926, 18–19.

Abraham, Mrs. (Rev.) "An Interesting Family." *York Pioneer and Historical Society*. Address of 1909: 24–29.

Adam, G. Mercer. *Toronto Old and New*. Toronto: The Mail Printing Co., 1891.

Adamson, Anthony. *Wasps in the Attic*. Toronto: A. Adamson, 1987.

Alfred, Rev. Brother. "Honourable John Elmsley: Legislative and Executive Councillor of Upper Canada." *Annual Report of the Canadian Catholic Historical Association*, 1936–37.

Arthur, Eric. *Toronto: No Mean City*. Revised by Stephen Otto. Toronto: University of Toronto Press, 1986.

Assessment Rolls, City of Toronto Archives.

"Bain Residence." *Canadian Homes and Gardens*, September 1938, 18–24.

Baker, Donna. *Moore Park: An Introductory History*. Toronto: Moore Park Residents' Association, 1984.

Baldwin, R. M. *The Baldwins and the Great Experiment*. Don Mills: Longmans, circa 1969.

Berchem, F. R. *The Yonge Street Story: 1793–1860*. Toronto: McGraw-Hill Ryerson, 1977.

Black, Conrad. "Conrad Black Remembers E. P. Taylor." *Financial Post*, 29 May 1989, 17.

Borough of East York. *Historic Buildings of East York*. East York, Ontario: Local Architectural Conservation Advisory Committee, circa 1984.

Boulton, D'Arcy. *Sketch of his Majesty's Province of Upper Canada*. London: Pickaby, 1805.

Boulton Genealogy. Special Collections, Metropolitan Toronto Reference Library.

Boulton, H. C. and W. S. Boulton. *Atlas of the City of Toronto*. Toronto: C. E. Goad, 1858.

Boyer, Barbaranne. *The Boardwalk Album: Memories of the Beach*. Erin, Ontario: Boston Mills Press, 1985.

Breakenridge, Mary Warren Baldwin. "Some account of the settlement in Canada of Robert Baldwin 'the emigrant' by a grand-daughter." Public Archives of Canada. 1859.

Browne, John Owensworth. *Map of the Township of York*. 1851.

———. *Plan of the City of Toronto*. 1862.

Bull, William Perkins. *Spadunk* or *From Paganism to Davenport United*. Toronto: Perkins Bull Foundation, circa 1935.

Campbell, Mary and Barbara Myrvold. *The Beach in Pictures* (Local History Handbook No. 6). Toronto: Toronto Public Library Board, , 1988.

Canadian Biographical Dictionary, The. Toronto: American Biographical Publishing Company,1880.

Cane, James. *Topographical Plan of the City and Liberties*. 1842.

Careless, J. M. S. *Toronto to 1918: An Illustrated History*. Toronto: James Lorimer, 1984.

Casa Loma: Canada's Famous Castle. Toronto: Kiwanis Club of West Toronto, 1938.

Chadwick, Edward Marion. *Ontarian Families*. Lambertville, Nova Scotia: Hunterdon House, 1970.

Colborne Lodge. Toronto: Women's Canadian Historical Society of Toronto, 1980.

Commemorative Biographical Record of the County of York, Ontario. Toronto: J.H. Beers & Co., 1907.

Cooper, John A. ed. *Men of Canada*. Toronto: Canadian Historical Co., 1901–1902.

Cotterell, Alfred T. *Map of Yorkville and its Vicinity*. 1878.

Crowder, Norman K. *Inhabitants of Toronto, Ontario. 1846*. Toronto: Ontario Genealogical Society, 1993.

Cruikshank, E. A. and A. F. Hunter, eds. *The Correspondence of the Honourable Peter Russell*. 3 vols. Toronto: Ontario Historical Society, 1932–36.

Dendy, William and William Kilbourn. *Toronto Observed: Its Architecture, Patrons and History*. Toronto: Oxford University Press, 1986.

Dendy, William. *Lost Toronto: Images of the City's Past*. Toronto: McLelland & Stewart, 1993.

Denison, George Taylor. *Recollections of a Police Magistrate*. Toronto: Musson Book Co., 1920.

Denison, John. *Casa Loma and the Man Who Built It*. Erin, Ontario: Boston Mills Press, 1982.

Denison, Richard Lonton. *The Canadian Pioneer Family of County York, England and County York, Ontario*. Toronto: n.p., 1951.

Denison, Robert Evelyn. *A History of the Denison Family of Canada 1792–1910*. Grimsby, Ontario: R. E. Denison, 1910.

Dictionary of Canadian Biography. Toronto: University of Toronto Press, 1983.

Duff, J. Clarence. *Pen Sketches of Historic Toronto*. Toronto: n.p., 1967.

Eaton, Flora McCrae. *Memory's Wall: The Autobiography of Flora McCrae Eaton*. Toronto: Clarke Urwin, 1956.

Edwards, F. "Small Town Big Men." *Maclean's*. 15 September 1939, 16–17, 23–25.

Encyclopaedia of Canadian Biography. Toronto: Canadian Press Syndicate, 1905.

Filey, Mike. *Toronto Sketches: The Way We Were*. Toronto: Dundurn, 1992.

———. *More Toronto Sketches: The Way We Were*. Toronto: Dundurn, 1993.

Firth, Edith. *Toronto in Art*. Toronto: Fitzhenry & Whiteside and City of Toronto, 1983.

———. *The Town of York: 1793–1815*. Toronto: The Champlain Society, 1962.

———. *The Town of York: 1815–34*. Toronto: The Champlain Society, 1966.

Fleming, Sir Sandford. *Topographical Plan of the City of Toronto*. 1851.

Fort-Menares, A. *A Directory to Historic Buildings in North York*. North York, Ontario: North York Historical Board, 1984.

Fulton, Albert and Keith Miller, eds. *The Art of Wychwood: An Exhibition of Art and Photography*. Toronto: Wychwood Park Archives, 1988.

Gagan, Paul. *The Denison Family of Toronto*. Toronto: University of Toronto Press, 1973.

Gentilcore, R. Louis and C. Grant Head. *Ontario's History in Maps*. Toronto: University of Toronto Press, 1984.

Gianelli, Adele. "Annandale, Country Estate of Dr. Herbert Bruce." *Canadian Homes and Gardens*. November 1927, 27–29, 76.

———. "Glendon Hall — Country Estate of E. R. Wood, Esq." *Canadian Homes and Gardens*. September 1926, 24–26, 60.

———. "The Tranquil Gardens of Ardwold." *Canadian Homes and Gardens*. July 1928, 26–27, 60.

Goad, Charles E. *Atlas of the City of Toronto and Vicinity*. Montreal: n.p., circa 1884.

Goldring, Madeline Ann. *The Denison Family of County York, England and County York, Ontario*. Ridgeville, Ontario: n.p., 1986.

"The Grange, Toronto." *The Canadian Architect and Builder* 12:2 (February 1900): 25–27.

Greenberg, Ken. "Toronto: The Unknown Grand Tradition." *Trace*. April–June 1981, 37–46.

"Grey Stone Crowns Emerald Lawns." *Canadian Homes and Gardens*. April 1936, 28–29.

Hart, Patricia. *Pioneering in North York*. Toronto: General Publishing, 1968.

Hathaway, E. J. *Jesse Ketchum and His Times*. Toronto: McLelland & Stewart, 1929.

Historical Board of Toronto. Inventory of Buildings of Architectural and Historical Importance. 1974.

History of Toronto and County of York, Ontario. Toronto: C. Blackett Robinson, 1885.

Hopkins, Jeanne. *The Henry Farm, Oriole: An Early Settlement of North York*. Willowdale: Henry Farm Community Interest Association, 1987.

———. "Looking Back." *North Toronto Post*. Various issues.

Howard, John G. *Incidents in the Life of J. G. Howard, Esq., of Colbourne Lodge, High Park*. Toronto: Copp, Clark & Co., 1885.

Illustrated Historical Atlas of the County of York (1878). Toronto: Peter Martin Associates Ltd., 1969.

Ingolfsrud, Elizabeth. "Private Lives." *Century Home*. October 1990, 35–53.

Innis, Mary Quayle, ed. *Mrs. Simcoe's Diary*. Toronto: Macmillan, 1965.

Inventory of Heritage Properties. North York, Culture Branch, Parks and Recreation. 1994.

Ireland, John. "John H. Dunn and the Bankers." *Ontario History* 60:2 (March 1970): 83–100.

Jackes, Lyman B. *Tales of North Toronto*. Toronto: Canadian Historical Press, 1948.

Jarvis, Julia. *In Good Faith*. Toronto: Julia Jarvis, 1976.

Jarvis, Mary Hoskin. *Historical Street Names of Toronto*. Toronto: Women's Canadian Historical Society of Toronto, 1931–34.

John Scarlett (of York) and Mary Thomson and Their Descendants. N.p., 1990.

Johnston, Hugh. *A Merchant Prince: Life of Hon. Senator John Macdonald*. Toronto: William Briggs, 1893.

Jones, Donald. "The House that Vaughan Built." *Toronto Star*. 9 October 1982, G14.

———. "How a Sweeping Passion Found its Home." *Toronto Star*. 14 September 1985, M3.

———. "Larratt Smith's Summerhill Connection." *Toronto Star*. 19 April 1986. M3.

———. "The Rise and Fall of a Gallant and Distinguished Officer." *Toronto Star*. 27 May 1984, M4.

———. "Thousands Heard Sifton's Call and Settled the Canadian West." *Toronto Star*. 27 November 1982, G26.

Kilbourn, William. *Toronto Remembered: A Celebration of the City*. Toronto: Stoddart, 1984.

Kingstone, Frederick William. *An Appeal In the Privy Council*. London: n.p., 1891.

Kinsella, Joan C. *A Walking Tour of the Old Deer Park Farm Area*. Toronto: Toronto Public Library, Deer Park Branch; 1984.

———. *Historical Walking Tour of Deer Park*. Toronto: Toronto Public Library Board, 1996.

Kiwanis Club. *Major General Sir Henry Mill Pellatt CVO, DCL, VD: A gentleman of Toronto, 1859–1939*. Toronto: Ontario Publishing Company, Ltd., 1942.

Kluckner, Michael. *Toronto, the Way It Was*. Toronto: Whitecap, 1988.

Kos-Rabcewicz-Zubkowski, Ludwik and William Edward Greening. *Sir Casimir Stanislaus Gzowski: A Biography*. Toronto: Burns and MacEachern, 1959.

Kyte, E. C. *Old Toronto*. Toronto: Macmillan, 1954.

"Lawrence Park Estates" brochure. Toronto: Dovercourt Land, Building and Savings Co., 1910.

Lawrence Park Estates: The Perfect Site of Ideal Homes. Toronto: Dovercourt Land, Building and Savings Co., 1911.

Laycock, Margaret and Barbara Myrvold. *Parkdale in Pictures: Its Development to 1889* (Local History Handbook No. 7). Toronto: Toronto Public Library Board, 1991.

Lennox, Muriel. *E. P. Taylor: A Horseman and his Horses*. Toronto: Burns & MacEachern, 1976.

Litvak, Marilyn. *The Grange: A Gentleman's House in Upper Canada*. Toronto: Art Gallery of Ontario, 1988.

Local History Files. North York Public Library Canadiana Department.

Lownsbrough, John. *The Privileged Few*. Toronto: Art Gallery of Ontario, 1980.

MacPherson, Mary-Etta. "Donalda Farm — The Estate of Mrs. D. A. Dunlap." *Canadian Homes and Gardens*. May 1929, 23–27, 66.

"Macpherson Estate, Toronto." *The Canadian Architect and Builder* 18:208 (April 1905): 51–53.

Malone, Tom. "Jesse Ketchum II in Upper Canada." *Canadian Theses on Microfiche*. Ottawa: National Library of Canada, 1979.

Map of the Village of Yorkville and Vicinity. Toronto: Copp, Clark and Co. 1871.

Mapping Toronto's First Century (exhibit catalogue). Toronto: Royal Ontario Museum, 1984.

Martyn, Lucy Booth. *Aristocratic Toronto: 19th Century Grandeur*. Toronto: Gage, 1980.

———. *100 Years of Grandeur: The Inside Stories of Toronto's Great Homes and the People Who Lived There*. Toronto: Pagurian, 1978.

———. *Original Toronto*. Sutton West, Ontario: The Paget Press, 1983.

McHugh, Patricia. *Toronto Architecture: A City Guide*. Toronto: McLelland & Stewart, 1989.

McRae, Marion, and Anthony Adamson. *The Ancestral Roof: Domestic Architecture of Upper Canada*. Toronto: Clarke Irwin, 1963.

Meredith, Alden G. *Mary's Rosedale and Gossip of Little York*. Ottawa: Graphic Publishers, 1928.

Middleton, Jesse Edgar. *The Municipality of Toronto: A History*. Toronto: Dominion Publishing Group, 1923.

Miles, Joan, ed. *West Toronto Junction Revisited: Excerpts from the Writings of A.B. Rice*. Erin, Ontario: West Toronto Junction Historical Society, 1986.

Miller, Jim. *The Founding of the Donalda Club*. Donalda Club, 1984.

Miller, Keith M. O. *The History and Development of Wychwood Park, 1888–1981*. Toronto: Wychwood Park Archives, 1981.

Moon, Lynda , Barbara Myrvold and Elizabeth Ridler. *Historical Walking Tour of Lawrence Park*. Toronto: Toronto Public Library Board and the North Toronto Historical Society, 1994.

Moranz, Jack. "H. R. Bain," *Star Weekly*. 3 September 1938, 52.

Myrvold, Barbara. *Bibliography of North Toronto*. Toronto: University of Toronto, 1973.

———. *Historical Walking Tour of Kensington Market and College Street*. Toronto: Toronto Public Library Board, 1992.

———. *Historical Walking Tour of the Danforth.* Toronto: Toronto Public Library Board, 1992.

Newman, Peter C. "A Baron Who Was Larger than Life." *Maclean's.* 29 May 1989, 44.

———. *The Canadian Establishment.* Toronto: McClelland & Stewart, 1975.

North Toronto in Pictures: 1889–1912. Toronto: Toronto Public Library Board, 1974.

Oreskovich, Carlie. *Sir Henry Pellatt: The King of Casa Loma.* Toronto: McGraw-Hill Ryerson, 1982.

Patterson, Cynthia, Carol MacDougall and George Levin. *Bloor–Dufferin in Pictures* (Local History Handbook No. 5). Toronto: Toronto Public Library Board, 1988.

"Penryn." *Canadian Homes and Gardens.* March 1938, 13, 22–23.

"'Penryn,' Perry Residence." *Canadian Homes and Gardens.* January–February 1935, 19.

"Previews: Bain Residence." *Canadian Homes and Gardens.* May 1937, 20–21.

Reed, T. A. "The Historic Value of Street Names." *Ontario Historical Society Papers and Records* 25 (1929): 385–87.

———. Scrapbooks in Special Collections, Metropolitan Toronto Reference Library. Twelve volumes.

———. "The Scaddings: a pioneer family in York." *Ontario Historical Society Papers and Records* 36 (1944): 7–20.

Riddell, William Renwick. *The Life of William Dummer Powell.* Lansing, Michigan: Michigan Historical Commission, 1924.

Ridout, Thomas. *Ten Years of Upper Canada in Peace and War 1805–1815.* Toronto: William Briggs, 1890.

Ritchie, Don. *North Toronto.* Erin, Ontario: Boston Mills Press, 1992.

Robertson, John Ross. *Landmarks of Toronto.* 1894. Reprint, Belleville, Ontario: Mika, 1976.

———. Photograph Collection, Metropolitan Toronto Reference Library.

Robinson, Sir Charles Walker. *Biography of J.B. Robinson.* Toronto: Morang & Co., 1904.

Rohmer, Richard H. *E. P. Taylor: The Biography of Edward Plunkett Taylor.* Toronto: McClelland & Stewart, 1978.

Rose, George Maclean, ed. *A Cyclopaedia of Canadian Biography.* Toronto: Rose Publishing, 1886.

Rust-D'Eye, George H. *Cabbagetown Remembered.* Erin, Ontario: Boston Mills Press, 1984.

Saunders, Guy. "Woodlawn." *York Pioneer.* 1972, 42–47.

Sauriol, Charles. *Remembering the Don: A Rare Record of Earlier Times Within the Don River Valley.* Scarborough: Consolidated Amethyst Communications, 1981.

Scadding, Dr. Henry. "The Story of Castle Frank." Address to the Pioneer Historical Society of the County of York. 7 May 1895.

———. *Toronto of Old.* 1873. Reprint. Abridged and edited by F. H. Armstrong. Toronto: Oxford University Press, 1966.

Sewell, John. *The Shape of the City: Toronto Struggles with Modern Planning.* Toronto: University of Toronto Press, 1993.

Shostack, Hannah and Christopher Webster. *The Summerhill Area: Historical Notes.* Toronto, 1974.

Smith, D. W. Sketch Map of York, 1794.

Smith, Goldwin. *Reminiscences.* Edited by Arnold Haultain. New York: Macmillan, 1910.

Speisman, Stephen A. "The Development of the Annex to the Mid-1920s" (typescript). 1978.

"Strath Gowan: The Southern Annex to Lawrence Park" brochure. Toronto: Dover Court Land, Building and Savings Co., 1912.

The Story of Colborne Lodge. Toronto: Ryrie Bros., 1905.

A Study of Rusholme Road. Toronto Region Architectural Conservancy. Toronto: 1991.

Thompson, Austin Seton. *Jarvis Street: A Story of Triumph and Tragedy.* Toronto: Personal Library Publishers, 1980.

———. *Spadina: A Story of Old Toronto.* Toronto: Pagurian, 1975.

Timperlake, James. *Illustrated Toronto: Past and Present.* Toronto: Peter A. Gross, 1877.

Toronto Board of Trade. *A Souvenir.* Toronto: Sabston Lithographing and Publishing Co., 1893.

Toronto: A City of Beautiful Homes. Toronto: Press Publishing, circa 1910.

Toronto Illustrated, 1893. Toronto: Ontario Genealogical Society, 1992.

Toronto Public Library, Branch Local History Files

Toronto Public Library Scrapbooks, Metropolitan Toronto Refence Library.

Tremaine, George. *Tremaine's Map of the County of York, Canada West.* 1860.

Wallace, Elisabeth. *The Grange and Its Occupants: The Boultons and Goldwin Smith.* Toronto: Art Gallery of Ontario, 1969.

Wallace, W. Stewart and W. A. MacKay. *The Macmillan Dictionary of Canadian Biography.* 9th Edition. Toronto: Macmillan, 1978.

Wood, Herbert Fairlie Wood. *Forgotten Canadians.* Toronto: Longmans, 1963.

York Home District. Transcript of a map showing earliest land grants in York Township, circa 1800.

York Pioneer and Historical Society Reports. Various years.

ARCHIVES AND FAMILY PAPERS:

A. O. Horwood Collection

Baldwin Family land records

Dinnick Family papers

Eaton Family papers

Elizabeth Russell correspondence

John George Howard journal and time book

Powell Family papers

Robert Baldwin papers

Samuel Peters Jarvis correspondence

W. W. Baldwin papers

INDEX